KB264691

Gödel and Cognitive Science

Gödel and Cognitive Science

ⓒ 2012 by Woosik Hyun

All right reserved.

No part of this book may be reproduced in any form

without the prior permission in writing of the author.

Printed in Korea

Author / Woosik Hyun

Dong Yeon Press

Address / #472-11, Mangwon-Dong, Mapo-Gu, Seoul 121-230 Korea

Phone / + 82 2 335-2630

Fax. / + 82 2 335-2640

e-mail / s-0609@hanmail.net

Printed / Oct. 30, 2012

ISBN 978-89-6447-189-0 94170

Price ₩15,000(13.50 USD)

Gödel and Cognitive Science

Woosik Hyun

Dong Yeon

Contents

Preface

Trying to understand perception by studying only neurons is like trying to understand bird flight by studying only feathers.

(David Marr, 1982)

In this volume it will be demonstrated what Gödel's celebrated incompleteness theorems and mathematical models in cognitive science emerges. We are concerned with meta-mathematical considerations about cognitive science. Thus, we ask: What is the computability of cognitive systems? How then do we understand what Gödel's incompleteness theorems imply in cognitive systems? How do we acquire the definition of cognition from the cognitive systems? How do we determine what is the equivalence of human mind and artificial mind?

In order to reconstruct the topics, it is necessary first to address three main cognitive systems from the meta-mathematical perspectives: the mind, the brain, and the machine. The notion of the mind used here is as follows: Let

M be the mind, B be the brain, and C be the computing machine, referred to as "computer". Then a mathematical product of two objects B and C is an object M and two mappings, connectionist approach c and symbolic approach s, are such that

$$B \xleftarrow{c} M \xrightarrow{s} C.$$

In this diagram, c and s are mathematical projections of M. Thus, they allow the construction of mappings into M from separate mappings f and g into B and C respectively. For an artificial mind A_i $(i = 1, 2, 3, ...)$,

$$B \xleftarrow{f} A_i \xrightarrow{g} C.$$

Given two mappings f and g, there is a mapping h such that $A_i \xrightarrow{h} M$, where $M = B \times C$ (that is, the mind is said to be a product of the brain and the computer). Hence, the mapping h can be characterized in terms of f and g without mention of all the elements in A_i.

Our methodology is metamathematical. This statement would say that the methodology not only transcendends mathematics but outclasses it. From this perspective, we are having some advantages:

First, when we give a definition of a formal system, there then arises the scientific possibility of generalizing or varying

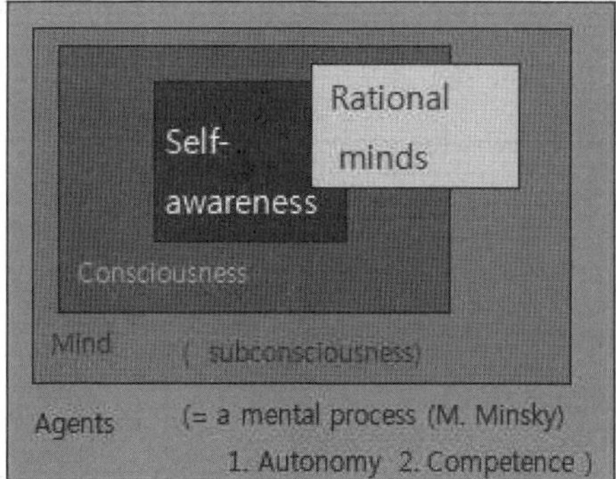

Figure 1. Varieties of Mind

the systems in the definition;

Second, although the formal approach is clearly devised by human cognition to represent certain objects, it is bound to be artificial. Thus, this formal study could provide a methodological bridge between the human and the artifact.

Neural network theory has been strongly pursued in response to the theory of Turing machine and its variants. Turing's analysis, so called the classic approach, deals with cognition as a computation by Turing machines, as if the mind were equivalent to a Turing machine. Neural network theorists claim that cognition cannot be understood in terms of Turing machine alone, but in dynamic relationships between neurons. This means that the mind-brain-machine problem exists not only inside Turing machine models but also among various neural network models.

In previous works of cognition, it is remarkable to note how little serious attention has been given to issues of the computability of neural networks with respect to Gödel's incompleteness theorems. To address a neural computability problem, we should investigate Gödel's disjunctive conclusion and then discuss metamathematical notions such as consistency and order of neural network models.

Some recurrent neural networks can be considered as higher-order formal systems. Hence one cannot prove its consistency in terms of first-order theories. The computability of neural networks may go beyond the computational incompleteness of Turing machines. If the mind is a recurrent neural network, more specifically, if cognition is a mapping of neural networks, then Gödel's incompleteness result does not limit the computational power of cognition.

Understanding implications of Gödel's theorems for cognitive systems requires that one looks back to Gödel's own interpretation of artificial cognition. According to Gödel's disjunctive conclusion, his incompleteness theorems imply neither the mechanism nor the mind-over-machine thesis. Rather his incompleteness theorems demonstrate an essential property that cognition in either the human or the artifact should obtain. However, this does not mean that the human mind is free from Gödel's incompleteness theorems.

Gödel's incompleteness theorems limit both human and artificial cognition in terms of the Turing machine models, whereas the theorems do not limit these two types of cognition in terms of the neural network models. That is to say, the neural network model implies a metacomputability that establishes an ever higher order by adding new formulas such as a Gödel proposition. Thus, Gödel's incompleteness theorems show that the superiority of neural computability over Turing computability is the very computational power of cognition.

This approach would provide some contributions to the foundations of cognitive science. First, it may enhance the formal understanding of cognition and provide a new basis for cognitive computability with regard to the neural network and Gödel's incompleteness theorems. Second, it may provide the reader with new results in the mind-brain-machine equivalence controversy. Third, it may serve as a new source of reference for Gödel's own view on the mind and machines. In all, it may provide a new perspective on the relationship between Gödel's incompleteness theorems and cognitive science. What I believe, consequently, is that cognitive science explores the metamathematical property of the mind as a brain-computer unit.

This book is a revision of my lecture notes and doctoral dissertation. For all the help, I would like to thank the Daewoo Foundation and the Department of Mathematical Science at the University of Memphis. I am deeply indebted to Professors Yillbyung Lee, Haseo Ki, Seungchong Lee, Seungsoo Park, Max Garzon and President Ilku Kang. Thanks are also due to my teachers: Sungsa Hong, Joongsuk Suh, Changkyun Park, Joohee Jeong, Seungon Lee, Byunghan Kim, Chansup Chung, Jungmo Lee, Stan Franklin, Michael Arbib, Robert Soare, Solomon Feferman and Roger Penrose. I would like to acknowledge my gratitude to my mentor Professor Taidong Han for his continual help and encouragement. Lastly, my sincere thanks go to Youngho Kim at Dong Yon Press.

Woosik Hyun

Glossary of the Symbols

'*A*', '*B*' are letters for propositions or formulas and '*A*(*x*)' is a propositional function of x or a formula with free variable '*x*'

Conjunction("*A* and *B*"): $A \wedge B$

Disjunction("*A* or *B*"): $A \vee B$

Negation("not *A*"): $\neg A$

Conditional, or *Implication*("if *A* then *B*"): $A \rightarrow B$

Biconditional("*A* if and only if *B*"): $A \leftrightarrow B$, $A \equiv B$

Universal quantification("for all x, *A*(*x*)"): $\forall x A(x)$

Existential quantification("there exists an x such that *A*(*x*)"): $\exists x A(x)$

Provability relation("*A* is provable in the system *S*"): $S \vdash A$

Satisfaction relation("*A* is satisfied in the model *M*"): $M \models A$

CHAPTER 1

Cognitive Science

While physics has been making matter less material,

psychology has been making mind less mental.

_Bertrand Russell

Scientific analysis of an object requires the context of mathematical models. Consequently, every model reflects the specific concerns and methods of its respective discipline. The development of computational models for studying cognition is extremely common these days and fundamental in cognitive science. Before discussing computational models, however, we need to be more specific about the theory of computability, which is a substantial branch of computer science and mathematical logic.

The origin of modern computability theories can be traced back to Kurt Gödel(1906-1978) in 1931 when he first introduced the concept of primitive recursive functions as proof of the celebrated incompleteness theorems. He also defined general recursion [Gödel 1934], which, during the 1930s, led to the various definitions of effective calculable functions by A. Church, S. Kleene, A. Turing, E. Post and others.

In particular, Gödel's results affected Turing's research on a formal model of a computing machine that would serve as an idealized human computer - what has come to be known as the Turing Machine. The Turing machine provided a precise description of computability [Turing 1936]. Turing's well known thesis states that if a function is definable by a finite mechanical procedure, then it is computable; that is, it can be computed by a Turing machine. The fundamental idea of both von Neumann's first computers and current digital computers is essentially based on Turing's formal computing machine [Kleene 1994; Davis 1987].

In 1943, W. McCulloch and W. Pitts introduced a network of formal neurons, consisting of threshold logic units, that showed how a formal model of the brain could simulate any universal Turing machine. This model is now regarded as the framework for artificial neural networks(hereafter referred to as 'neural networks'). Both the Turing machine and the neural network model have been the main models used in addressing the most fundamental question in cognitive science: Can artificial minds think like the human mind? No cognitive scientist can be free from the landmarks of Gödel, Turing, McCulloch and Pitts.

The computability theory of neural networks is not just one more issue among many to be debated in cognitive science, but rather one of the most important underlying issues. An analysis of neural computability could provide a better understanding of cognition in humans and in artifacts. It is remarkable to observe, however, how little serious attention has been given to the theme of neural computability and Gödel's incompleteness in cognitive science.

Nevertheless, we have to caution ourselves in that the world of formal science deals with the formal relationship between real objects, whereas empirical science is concerned with the real objects themselves. It is expedient, therefore, for us to perceive the object as being nothing more than a conceptual guide in our search for the theory that would be most appropriate for cognitive science.

1.1 Cognition as Mapping

One of the most fundamental difficulties for cognitive scientists is to define cognition or, more precisely, to define the scope of cognition. In a broader sense, the term *cognition* may be defined differently according to the field concerned. In psychology, cognition is defined as a mental function in a mental world. In neuroscience, it is defined as a physical function in a biological world and, in artificial intelligence(AI), cognition is defined as a computational function in a mechanical world.

According to Arbib, the brain is the biological mechanism; the machine is the technological mechanism; and the mind is a subset of the function of the brain's activity([Arbib 1995]). On this, Penrose distinctly explains the mind, machine, and brain as being of in a mental world, a mathematical world, and a physical world, respectively([Penrose 1997]).

Cognitive scientist would unify cognition, with respect to the mind, the brain, and the machine, into a single frame. This does not mean that the three systems are not different from each other. Rather, cognition in the mind may be considered as a certain level of processing of the brain and the machine. For example, M. Minsky regarded the mind as the process or function of the brain([Minsky 1985]). According to him, minds are simply what brains do. For another example, A. Newell offered the description of the mind as the control system that guides the behaving organism in its interactions with the dynamic real world([Newell 1990]). Since the definition seems more appropriate to the brain, I would agree with Arbib that such a definition does not distinguish the mind from the brain([Arbib 1993]).

Cognition can be seen as an action of knowing, or a faculty of the mind. In general, cognition is distinguished from emotion and covers the concepts of awareness, intelligence, intuition, personal acquaintance, recognition, skill, and understanding([Benjafield 1992]). Cognition has typical features such as perception, learning, memory, thinking and language. Thus, contemporary cognitive scientists generally assume cognition to be a collection of goal-oriented behaviors such as reasoning, learning, language processing, problem solving among others.

The boundary, however, is flexible([Newell 1990, 1992]). Newell contends that cognition broadly covers problem solving, decision making, routine action, memory, learning, skill, perception, motor activity, language, motivation, emotion, imagining, dreaming, etc... *Cognition* has no single precise definition or well-defined description and, therefore, offers no uniform scope. According to Newell, intelligence is a subset of cognition since intelligence does not include the symbol level([Newell 1990]). Here, however, we will use two terms interchangeably. What is commonly needed for the science of cognition is a much richer concept of knowledge representation and knowledge process.

Most significantly, cognition is regarded as a concept of computation. For example, J. Haugeland maintained that the computational view of thought has become the single most important theoretical hypothesis in psychology([Haugelnad 1981]). D. Dennett asserted that a non-question-begging psychology must be computational([Dennett 1978]). D. Marr stated that Chomsky's notion of a competence theory for English syntax captures the idea of what it means to have a computational theory for that specific problem([Marr 1977]). Computation has been a key word and methodology for constituting theories of cognition([Pylyshyn 1984; 1989]). Following Marr, there are two important concepts for understanding cognition: representation and process([Marr 1982]).

REPRESENTATION. A *representation* is defined as a formal system for making explicit certain entities or types of information, together with a specification of how the system does this. For example, the Arabic, Roman and binary numeral systems are all formal systems for representing numbers.

PROCESS. A *process* is defined as a mapping from one formal system as representation to another.

Marr provided the significant frame of work for cognitive science. He suggested that there are three levels at which the cognitive process must be studied and that we should focus on computational theory. The three levels [Marr 1982] are as follows:

1. *Computational theory*: What is the goal of the computation, why is it appropriate, and what is the logic of the strategy by which it can be carried out?
2. *Representation* and *algorithm*: How can this computational theory be implemented? In particular, what is the repre-

sentation for the input and output, and what is the algorithm for the transformation?

3. *Hardware implementation*: How can the representation and algorithm be realized physically?

Philosophically, the relation between 1 and 2 is interpreted as type identity; the relation between 2 and 3 is as realization. Type identity is not always identified with realization([Horgan and Tienson 1996]).

We agree with Marr in terms of functional analysis, but we disagree with him in regard to structural analysis. For Marr's three levels of analysis cannot explain the relationship between behaviors and neurons. In other words, they do not provide a bridge between mental activities and brain regions.

On this point, Arbib's thesis of *schemas*(Figure 1.) is more convincing. According to Arbib, schemas are the units of computational analysis that intermediate between cognitive behaviors and physical neurons([Arbib 1989, 1992, 1993]). Hence, the concept of schemas mediates between two analyses: functional and structural, or high level and low level analysis, respectively.

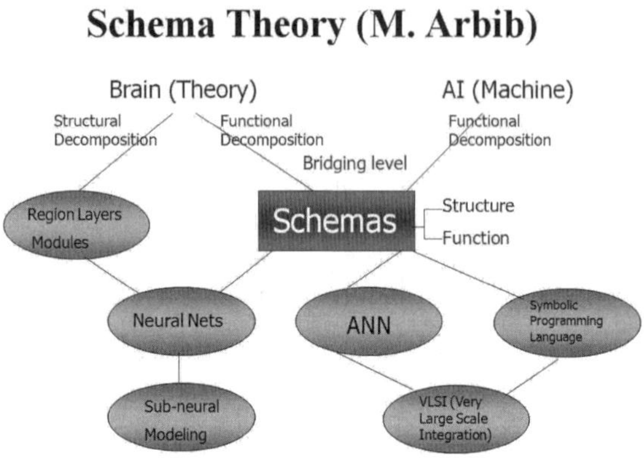

Schema Theory (M. Arbib)

Figure 1. Schema Theory

Cognition in this research refers to a kind of mapping. Thus, we may think of it as a formal mapping from a system of times to a system of spaces,

$$Time \xrightarrow{\;cognition\;} Space.$$

Thus, cognition is like a plexus of properties rather than a single concept. The properties of cognition include the progression of a modified model of the world with its attendant adaptability, flexibility and generality, and dynamic planning([Arbib 1989]). In this book, the domain of cognition is defined by a system of discrete times, and its range by a system of mental spaces, where mental spaces are restricted to the human mind.

Dynamical Hypothesis: Natural cognitive systems are dynamical and are thus best understood from the perspective of dynamics.

A *dynamical* system is one that changes in time; what changes is the state of the system. A mathematical dynamical system consists of the space of all states of the system and a rule called the dynamic for determining the state([Port & Van Gelder 1995]).

From a macro perspective, it would be desirable to have mathematical knowledge of cognition. This has several advantages for cognitive science because

1. The objects of computational models are mathematical.
2. The operations of computational models are mathematical.
3. The languages of computational models are mathematical.
4. The mathematical approaches may go beyond empirical limitations of time and space resources.

For a rigorous discussion on cognition, we will restrict its scope and level to that of mathematical thinking. Mathematical thinking among others is clearly a goal-oriented behavior and a higher mental process.

1.2 Cognitive Science

The new characteristic of cognitive science lies in the study of the mind with respect to both the brain and the machine. Therefore, we need to consider the wide range of the mind, the brain, and the machine in terms of cognitive science. Thus only a theory that is valid for all these systems can lead to a viable theory in cognitive science.

Cognitive science is an emerging field of study whose boundaries are not yet well-defined. According to Arbib, cognitive science is an umbrella term which unites three areas: *Artificial Intelligence* which studies how computers may be programmed to yield intelligent behavior without necessarily attempting to provide a correlation between structures in the program and structures in the brain; *Cognitive Psychology* which attempts to explain the mind in terms of information processing; and *Brain Theory* which seeks to enhance our understanding of human thought and the neural basis of human and animal behavior([Arbib 1985, 1995]).

D. Norman defines cognitive science as the search for understanding of cognition both in general and in the abstract, be it real or hypothetical, human or non-human, natural or artificial([Norman 1981]). According to the definition by H. Simon, cognitive science is the study of intelligence and intelligent systems, such as humans, computers and the abstract, with particular reference to intelligent behavior as computation([Simon & Kaplan 1989]).

We define cognitive science as the study of the union of symbolic and connectionist approaches. Since what we refer to as the human mind is regarded as a product of the human brain and the computing machine, we can obtain two mathematical projections: one being from the system of mind to the system of brains, called the *connectionist approach*; and the other from the system of mind to the system of computing machines, called the *symbolic approach.* Thus, the former is concerned with mind-as-computing brain, whereas the latter is concerned with mind-as-computing machine. The metaphors of the brain and the computer will be used, respectively, to designate these two approaches. Cognitive science has the assumption that we can learn about the mind from studying the relationship between the brain and the computing machine(computer).

From this assumption, we arrive at two models for an artificial mind: the Turing machine for the symbolic approach and the neural network for the connectionist one. Both models lead to the fundamental question in cognitive science: *How does one determine whether or not human cognition can be approached as artificial cognition?* This is the question that will be our primary focus with regard to the formal aspects of the computational model for the brain. In order to describe cognition more mathematically, we should specify how the meta-mathematical property of cognitive systems operates.

The methodology of cognitive science can be divided into two distinctive divisions: *theoretical* and *experimental.* One of the proper methodologies can be found in D. Marr and T. Poggio's paper [1979] *A Computational Theory of Human Stereo Vision.* In their work, they use (a) biological evidence, (b) formalization of problems and solutions, and (c) experiments.

Cognitive science was initially dominated by the symbolic approach, that is, serial processing or the information-processing paradigm; little attention was paid to the connectionist approach, that is, parallel processing. Since the 1980s, however, an increasing number of researchers in cognitive science have been concerned with neural modeling.

Symbolic Approach: Mapping from Mind to Machine

The term *symbolism* is used for studies that model human thought and behavior in terms of symbolic manipulation of sequential automaton-like units. The symbolic school views the mind as a serial symbolic manipulating system. According to Horgan and Tienson, symbolic view that cognition is realized by an algorithm over symbolic representations, i.e. by rule-governed symbol manipulation, involves three basic assumptions([Horgan & Tienson 1996]):

1. Intelligent cognition employs structurally complex mental representations.

2. Cognitive processing is sensitive to the structure of these representations(and thereby is sensitive to their content).

3. Cognitive processing conforms to precise, exceptionless rules, statable over the representations themselves and articulable in the format of a computer program. In particular, the rules mentioned in assumption 3 is called programable representation-level rules.

This machine-style theory of processing takes its inspiration from the Turing machine, which executes operations serially([Newell & Simon 1976; Fodor & Pylyshyn 1988]). According to Simon and Newell, a physical symbol system is a machine that produces through time an evolving collection of symbol structures. Simon and Newell formulated *the physical symbol system hypothesis* as an empirical hypothesis.

Physical Symbol System Hypothesis: A physical symbol system has the necessary and sufficient means for general intelligent action([Newell & Simon 1976]).

The term *necessary* refers to the fact that any physical system that exhibits general intelligence will be an instance of a physical symbol system. The term *sufficient* refers to the fact that any physical symbol system can be organized further to exhibit general intelligence. The term *general intelligent action* means the same scope of intelligence as we see in human action: that in real situations behavior appropriate to the ends of the system and adaptive to the demands of the environment can occur within some physical limits([Newell 1980]).

The term *physical* refers to two features: (1) such systems clearly obey the laws of physics - they are realizable by engineered systems made of engineered components; (2) the term *symbol* is not restricted to human symbol systems. Simon and Newell claimed that two notions are central to this structure of expressions, symbols, and objects: designation and interpretation.

DESIGNATION. An expression designates an object if, given the expression, the system can either affect the object itself or behave in ways dependent on the object.

INTERPRETATION. The system can interpret an expression if the expression designates a process and if, given the expression, the system can carry out the process.

Interpretation used here is a process that takes symbol structures, expressions, as input and execute operations([Newell 1990]). According to the symbolic school, the study of formal logic and computers leads to these notions and suggests that intelligence may reside in physical symbol systems.

Connectionist Approach: Mapping from Mind to Brain

Most of the computational models have been dominantly serial, whereas many properties of the human mind involve parallel processing. The term *connectionism* is used for studies that model human thought and behavior in terms of networks of neuron-like units working parallel and in distributed manner.

This connectionist school views cognitive systems as a parallel distributed processing system. This brain-style theory of processing takes its inspiration from the neural network, which executes all operations simultaneously in a parallel manner([Rumelhart & McClelland 1986; Smolensky 1988]). The following can be called as neural network hypothesis.

Neural Network Hypothesis: To psychology, however defined, specification of the net[work] would contribute all that could be achieved in that field - even if the analysis were pushed to the ultimate psychic units or psychons, for a psychon can be no less than the activity of a single neuron([McCulloch & Pitts 1943]).

Connectionism then may be characterized, as M. Arbib has suggested([Arbib 1987]):

1. The use of networks of active computing elements, with programs residing in the structure of interconnections.

2. The restriction of these elements to a simple structure. The proper structure for such a unit is evolving, but the element is more like a linear threshold unit or a McCulloch-Pitts neuron (perhaps augmented by a few numerical state variables and a noise term) than either a real neuron or a computer program of moderate complexity.

3. Massive parallelism, with no centralized control(other than control that can be exerted by other massively parallel networks).

4. The encoding of semantic units either by single network units or by patterns of activity in a population of such units.

Nonetheless, in the 1980s, there came to be increasing debate between the symbolic group and the connectionist group([Bobrow 1994; Bechtel & Abrahamsen 1991; Horgan & Tienson 1991; Cole, Fetzer & Rankin 1990]). We will not discuss this debate in detail here because the current approaches of the debate indicates that no cognitive scientist could totally deny the complementary success of the two approaches. Rather, both are different but compatible approaches for understanding the mind in various forms(for symbolic-connectionist models, see [Holyoak & Spellman 1993; Minsky 1991a; Dyer 1991]).

For more advanced understanding as a whole, we need to

consider cognition in terms of both connectionism and symbolism(Figure 2).

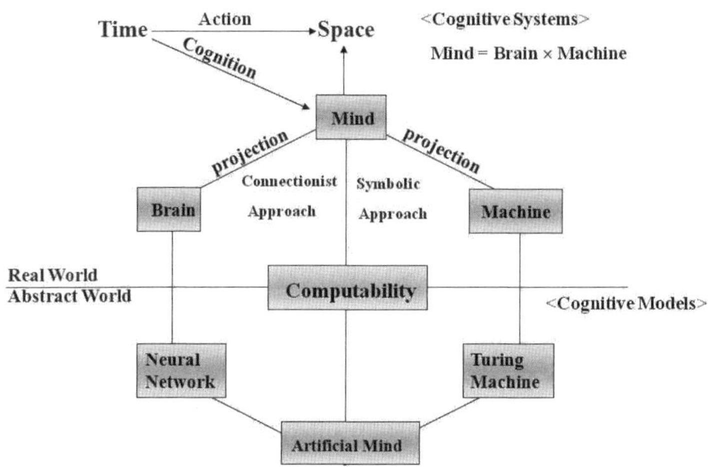

Figure 2. Cognitive Science

1.3 Theses for Cognitive Science

Computability theory is a substantial branch of mathematical logic and computer science that has greatly affected the mechanization of cognition. We also observe that modern formal logic, first-order logic, in particular, has been absolutely fundamental in providing a foundation for cognitive science in general, and for Artificial Intelligence research in particular.

Church's Thesis

The idea that human cognition may be reducible to computation is not a new one. G. W. von Leibniz imagined *characteristica universalis*, that is, a universal language of symbols into which any model of cognition could be translated. Followed by George Boole, who, in his 1854 work, *The Laws of Thought: The Mathematical Theories of Logic and Probabilities*, turned rules of thought into a system of algebraic logic. In his 1897 *Begriffsschrift*, Gottlob Frege devised a formal language and the predicate calculus for the expression of logical arguments. Finally, David Hilbert constructed the modern formal axiomatic system for the foundation of mathematics as well as the fulfillment of Leibniz's dream.

One of the fundamental contributions of mathematical logic to cognitive science is the precise formulation and study of the computable functions in a given system. This first came from Gödel's proof of incompleteness theorems. In the proof, Gödel defined and used primitive recursive functions that led, during the mid-1930's, to various definitions of computable functions by A. Church, S. C. Kleene, E. Post, and A. Turing. Mathematically, these are equivalent functions that could be calculated by a modern computer if we were to ignore the restrictions on computing time and storage capacity.

Computation is a process whereby we proceed from initially given objects, called *inputs*, through a series of steps according to a fixed set of rules, called a *program, procedure,* or *algorithm,* and arrive at the end of these steps with a final result, called the *output.* The algorithm, a set of rules proceeding from inputs to outputs, must be precise and definite, with each successive step clearly determined.

The concept of computability concerns those objects that may be specified in principle by computations. Since we confine the notion to computability on the natural numbers, the inputs, outputs, the program, and computation will be countable mathematical objects. Thus, we say that a number theoretic function is *computable* if and only if there is an algorithm or effective procedure for finding the value of the function on arbitrary given inputs.

DEFINITION. A function is *computable* or *effectively calculable* if it can be calculated by a finite mechanical procedure.

A function is *recursive* if it is *general recursive,* as defined by Gödel, which essentially, is to say that a function is general recursive if there is a *finite set of equations*([Gödel 1934]). Gödel indicated that recursive functions have the important property that, for each set of values of the arguments, the value of the function can be computed by a finite procedure. Gödel, however, pointed out a problem with the converse:

This cannot be proved, since the notion of finite computation is not defined, but it serves as a heuristic principle([Gödel 1934], 348).

Thus he was still not at all convinced that his definition was sufficiently inclusive([Davis 1982]).

Church's Thesis: The set of effectively calculable function is identical to the set of the recursive function.

Church-Markov-Turing Thesis: A partial function $\varphi: N^n \to N$ is computable if and only if it is computable by some binary Turing machine, that is, if and only if $\varphi = \varphi_k$ for some k. This is commonly known as Church's Thesis. However, this combinatory thesis comes from Church, Turing, and Markov, not from Church alone.

Church's thesis cannot be a mathematical theorem because its formulation involves the notion of the term *effectively calculable* in the intuitive sense. By this thesis, the class of non-recursive functions implies the class of non-computable functions. Thus, the acceptance of Church's thesis is useful in proving the non-existence of an algorithm and hence, the solvability of given algorithmic problems.

In his paper[Church 1936], Church maintained this thesis not in terms of his own notion, λ-*definability*, but rather in terms of Gödel's general recursion. Yet Gödel did not accept this thesis at the time because, he insisted, it was thoroughly unsatisfactory to define the effectively calculable function to be a particular class without first showing that the generally accepted properties of the notion of effective calculability necessarily lead to this class([Davis 1982]). Gödel's critique of Church's thesis is convincing(for the flaw in Church's thesis, see [Soare 1996]; [Sieg 1994]; [Davis 1982]).

It is remarkable to note that Gödel accepted Turing's analysis as the concept of computability rather than recursion, which he himself established; he never used the term *recursion* to mean *computability*.

Turing's Thesis

After Turing's work [1936], Gödel explicitly asserted that Turing's analysis and notion of computability was the correct definition of mechanical calculability and computability([Gödel 1964; 1951]). According to Gödel,

The most satisfactory way, in my opinion, is that of reducing the concept of finite procedure to that of a machine with a finite number of parts, as has been done by the British mathematician Turing([Gödel 1951], 305).

Turing's work gives an analysis of the concept of mechanical procedure(alias algorithm or computation procedure or finite combinatorial procedure). This concept is shown to be equivalent with that of a Turing machine([Gödel 1964,] 369).

It is remarkable that Gödel positively accepted Turing's thesis and analysis and, thereafter, always gave credit to Turing, not to Church([Sieg 1994], 88):

But I was completely convinced only by Turing's paper(Gödel: Letter to Kreisel of May 1, 1968).

Turing's Thesis: If a function is informally computable, that is, definable by a finite mechanical procedure or algorithm, then it is computable by a Turing machine.

Turing's Thesis says that every algorithm can be programmed on a one-tape Turing machine. By Turing's thesis, we obtain the following:

1. If a function is definable by a finite mechanical procedure, then it is computable by a Turing's idealized human computer.
2. If a function is effectively calculable, then it is computable by a Turing's idealized human computer.
3. If a function is calculable by a Turing's idealized human

computer, then it is Turing computable.

Turing analyzed an idealized human computing agent with the conception of a function produced by a mechanical procedure. The mechanical procedure is a simple formal device, now called a Turing machine. In terms of the mechanical procedure, he attempted to prove the equivalence of the idealized human computer and the computing machine.

Turing computability became fundamental for the theoretical conceptualization of modern general-purpose digital computers, as realized by Turing and von Neumann in the 1950s. Turing's analysis is a basis for cognitive science in that he began with modeling human cognition by carrying out a computation through a finite sequence of symbol manipulation.

Soare's Thesis

The notion of the computable and of the recursive have been used interchangeably, because the classes of the two properties are proved to be equivalent in an external sense. Based on a careful historical and mathematical analysis of computability and recursion, however, R. I. Soare asserts that there are essential differences between the concepts of *computability* and *recursion*([Soare 1996; 1999]). He emphasizes that computable should be considered as *Turing computable* rather than as recursion. He further argues that since *recursion* is defined only in terms of self-reference in *primitive recursion*, it does not cover the additional meaning of computable functions as defined by a Turing machine or its equivalents.

Primitive Recursion: Let C be the smallest class of primitive recursive functions. If $g,h \in C$ and $n \geq 1$ then $f \in C$ where

$$f(0, x_2, ..., x_n) = g(x_2, ..., x_n)$$
$$f(x_1 + 1, x_2, ..., x_n) = h(x_1, f(x_1, x_2, ..., x_n), x_2, ..., x_n)$$

assuming g and h are functions of $n-1$ and $n+1$ variables respectively.

I would call the following recommendations Soare's thesis.

Soare's Thesis.

1. The term *recursive* should no longer carry the additional meaning of *computable* or *decidable*.

2. If functions are defined, or sets are enumerated, or relative computability is defined using Turing machines, register machines, or variants of these, then the name *computable* rather than *recursive* should be attached to the result, as in [Cutland 1980]; [Davis 1958], [Boolos & Jeffrey 1974], [Soare 1987] and others.

3. We should distinguish between the intensional meaning of Church's Thesis(that all effectively calculable functions are general recursive) versus Turing's Thesis(that all intuitively computable functions are computable by a Turing machine). When we are writing a paper dealing with which classes of functions are Turing computable(i.e., mechanistic), as in [Gandy 1980] and in many other places, we should refer

to *Turing's Thesis*(as in [Sieg 1994] and [Tamburrini 1995]) not to *Church's Thesis*.

4. We should call the subject *Computability Theory* or simply *Computability* instead of *Recursive Function Theory* or *Recursion Theory*.

According to Soare's suggestion, the concept of computability implies the concept of recursion in the intensional sense. The concept of *computable* is associated with the notion of computation, algorithm, and with the functions defined by(or sets enumerated by) Turing machines, and also with relative Turing computability, whereas the concept of *recursive* is associated with: definition by recursion, general recursive functions in the sense in Herbrand-Gödel, fixed points as in the Kleene Recursion Theorem.

Let $\{P_n\}_{n \in N}$ be an effective listing of all Turing programs and let φ_n be the computable partial function computed by P_n. Then the Kleene Recursion Theorem says that for every Turing computable total function $f(x)$ there is a fixed point n such that $\varphi_{f(n)} = \varphi_n$([Soare 1987]).

Soare proposes that researchers distinguish between the intensional menaing of Church's Thesis(that all effectively calculable functions are general recursive) versus that of Turing's Thesis(that all intuitively computable functions are computable by a Turing machine)([Soare 1999]). I agree with Gödel and Soare in the sense that the notion of computability should be thought of as Turing computability rather than recursion.

CHAPTER 2

Gödel's Incompleteness Theorems

2.1 Formal Mathematical Systems

According to Gödel, a *formal mathematical system* is a system of symbols with rules for using them([Gödel 1934]). A *formal mathematical system* consists of two parts: a *formal language* that provides a precisely demarcated class of expressions called formulas, and *transformation rules* that have *axioms* and *rules of inference* and determine a specified class of formulas derivable in the formal system.

FORMAL LANGUAGE: The individual symbols are called *undefined terms*. *Formulas* are finite sequences of the undefined terms.

TRANSFORMATION RULE: There is a class of formulas called *meaningful formulas*, and a class of meaningful formulas called *axioms*. There may be a finite or infinite number of axioms. *Rule of inference* is a specified list of rules.

If such a rule be called *Rule*, it defines the relation of *immediate consequence* by *Rule* between a set of meaningful formulas $P_1, ..., P_k$ called the *premises* and a meaningful formula C, called the *conclusion*.

For each rule of inference there is a finite procedure for determining whether a given formula B is an immediate consequence by that rule of given formulas $A_1, .., A_n$, and there is a finite procedure for determining whether a given formula is a meaningful formula or an axiom. Therefore, rule of inference must be effective.

A formula C is called an *immediate consequence* of $P_1, ..., P_k$ if C is an immediate consequence of $P_1, ..., P_k$ by any one of the rules of inference. A finite sequence of formulas is a *proof*, that is, the last formula of the sequence, if each formula of the sequence is either an axiom or an immediate consequence of one or more of the preceding formulas. A formula is *provable* if a proof of it exists.

Let the symbol $\neg$ be one of the undefined terms and express negation. Then the formal system is said to be *complete* if for every meaningful formula A either A or $\neg A$ is provable. A formal system is said to be *consistent* if and only if there is no formula such that both A and $\neg A$ are provable. A formal system is said to be *decidable* if and only if there exists a mechanical procedure for determining whether any given formula is provable.

The Language of First-Order Formal Systems

A formal language of first-order formal system, L_1, is a finite set of symbols:

$$L_1 = \{c, ..., f, ..., R, ..., x, y, z, ..., \neg, \wedge, \vee, \rightarrow, \leftrightarrow, =, \forall, \exists, (,)\},$$

where $c, ...$ are constant symbols; $f, ...$ function symbols; $R, ...$ predicate symbols (called relation symbols); $x, y, z, ...$ variable symbols; $\neg$ (not), $\wedge$ (and), $\vee$ (or), $\rightarrow$ (implies), $\leftrightarrow$ (if and only if) logical connectives; $=$ the equality symbol; $\forall$ (for all), $\exists$ (there exists) quantifiers ; and $(,)$ parentheses.

A formal language of second-order system, L_2, is L_1 augmented with second-order variables that range over functions and relations. Thus, unlike the first-order language, second-order formal system allows one to quantify over subsets of the universe of discourse U and functions $f: U^n \rightarrow U$. In this sense, the second-order formal system has a stronger power of expression than the first-order formal system.

The Syntax of First-Order Formal Systems

Any finite sequence is called an *expression*. From the set of expressions, we form grammatically correct statements of L_1 as well-formed formulas (*wff*) consisting of terms, atomic formulas, and formulas.

DEFINITION. Let L_1 be a first-order language. Then

1. *Terms* of L_1 are defined as follows:

1) Every variable and constant is a term.

2) If f is an n-ary function symbol and $t_1,...,t_n$ are terms, then $f(t_1,...,t_n)$ is a term.

2. *Atomic formulas* of L_1 are defined as follows:

1) If s and t are terms, then $(s = t)$ is an atomic formula.

2) If R is an n-ary relation symbol and $t_1,...,t_n$ are terms, then $R(t_1,...,t_n)$ is an atomic formula.

3. *Formulas* of L_1 are defined as follows:

1) Every atomic formula is a formula,

2) If A and B are formulas so are $\neg A$, $(A \wedge B)$, $(A \vee B)$, $(A \to B)$ and $(A \leftrightarrow B)$.

3) If A is formula and x is a variable, then so are $\forall x A$ and $\exists x A$.

DEFINITION. A first-order *statement*(or *sentence*) of L_1 is a formula with no free variables.

DEFINITION. 1. A *proof*(or *derivation*) is a finite sequence of formulas such that each formula in the sequence either is an axiom or else results by a rule of inference from formulas that precede it in the sequence.

2. A formula is *provable*(or *derivable*) if and only if there is a proof of it. We write

$$S \vdash A$$

for "a formula A is provable in a formal system S".

DEFINITION. Let S be a formal system. Then

1. S is *consistent* if and only if the statement $A \wedge \neg A$ cannot be provable in S for any A.

2. S is *syntactically complete* if and only if for every statement either A is provable or else $\neg A$ is provable in S.

3. S is *decidable* if and only if there is a mechanical procedure for determining whether any given formula is provable in S.

4. For any function f, f is *computable* by a Turing machine if and only if f is representable in S, if S is consistent.

The Semantics of First-Order Formal Systems

Semantics is the study of interpretations of formal model, and of properties of symbols that are defined with respect to a universe of discourse, whereas *syntax* is the study of proof of formal system, and of the purely formal properties of symbols with no mention of interpretations.

DEFINITION. A *structure* (or *model*) for the first-language L_1 is a pair $M = (U, I)$, where U is the universe of M and I is the interpretation function which maps the symbols of L_1 to appropriate constants, functions, and relations in U such that

1. If $c \in L_1$ is a constant symbol, then $I(c) \in U$.

2. If $f \in L_1$ is an n-ary function symbol, then $I(f): U^n \to U$.

3. If $R \in L_1$ is an n-ary relation symbol, then $I(R) \subseteq U^n$.

An *assignment* in M is a function α from the set of variables of L_1 to the universe U. Thus, α assigns a meaning $\alpha(x)$ to the variable x. Then we define a relation, for every assignment and every formula A in U,

$$M \vDash A[\alpha]$$

(read: the assignment satisfies the formula A in M, or M satisfies A with α).

DEFINITION. Let M be a model for L_1 and $\bar{\alpha}$ be a function from a set of terms to U. Then, the definition of satisfaction of well-formed formulas is as follows:

1. *Terms*

1) If t is a constant symbol c, then $\bar{\alpha}(t) = c$.

2) If t is a variable symbol x, then $\bar{\alpha}(t) = \alpha(x)$.

3) If t is the term $f(t_1,...,t_n)$,

then $\bar{\alpha}(f(t_1,...,t_n)) = f(\bar{\alpha}(t_1), .., \bar{\alpha}(t_n))$.

2. *Atomic formulas*

1) $M \vDash (t_1 = t_2)[\alpha]$ if and only if $\bar{\alpha}(t_1) = \bar{\alpha}(t_2)$.

2) $M \vDash R(t_1,..,t_n)[\alpha]$ if and only if $(\bar{\alpha}(t_1),...,\bar{\alpha}(t_n)) \in R$.

3. *Formulas*

1) $M \vDash \neg A[\alpha]$ if and only if $M \nvDash A[\alpha]$.

2) $M \vDash (A \wedge B)[\alpha]$ if and only if $M \vDash A[\alpha] \wedge M \vDash B[\alpha]$.

3) $M \vDash (A \vee B)[\alpha]$ if and only if $M \vDash A[\alpha] \vee M \vDash B[\alpha]$.

4) $M \vDash (A \rightarrow B)[\alpha]$ if and only if $M \vDash A[\alpha] \rightarrow M \vDash B[\alpha]$.

5) $M \vDash (A \leftrightarrow B)[\alpha]$ if and only if $M \vDash A[\alpha] \leftrightarrow M \vDash B[\alpha]$.

6) $M \vDash \forall x A(x,u_1,...,u_n)[\alpha]$ if and only if for all $u \in U$, $M \vDash \forall A(u,u_1,...,u_n)[\alpha]$.

7) $M \vDash \exists x A(x,u_1,...,u_n)[\alpha]$ if and only if there exists a $u \in U$, $M \vDash \exists A(u,u_1,...,u_n)[\alpha]$.

DEFINITION. Let M and N be models for L_1. Then

1. M and N are *logically equivalent* if and only if for all statements A of L_1,

$$M \vDash A \leftrightarrow N \vDash A.$$

2. If M and N are *isomorphic* then two model are equivalent.

By a theory T in L_1 we mean a set of statements of L_1 such that for any statement A, $A \in T$ if $T \vDash A$. The notion $M \vDash T$, read M is a model of theory T, means that M is a structure for L_1 such that M satisfies every formula $A \in T$. M is model for a set of statements if all the statements are true in M. Therefore, for a structure

M, the theory of M, $Th(M)$, is the set of all sentences true in M.

DEFINITION. Let T be a theory in L_1. Then

1. T is *consistent* if the statement $A \wedge \neg A$ cannot be proved from T for any A.

2. If $A \in T$ is a *valid* statement, it is true in every model.

3. If T has a model, then it is consistent.

THEOREMS. Let T be any consistent set of statements and M be a model for T. Then

1. [Gödel's Completeness]. There exists a model for T whose cardinality does not exceed the cardinality of the number of statements in T if T is infinite, and is countable if T is finite.

2. [Completeness] If a statement A is true in every model M, then A is provable in T.

3. [Soundness] If a statement A is provable in T, then there is a model M of A.

4. [Compactness]. If every finite subset of T has a model, then T has a model.

5. [Löwenheim-Skolem]. There is a submodel of M such that $|U| \leq (|T|, \aleph_0)$, that is, whose cardinality does not exceed that of T if T is infinite and is at most countable if T is finite.

Herbrand-Gödel-Kleene System

The Hebrand-Gödel-Kleene system HGK is a finite set of equations defined by the following:

THE LANGUAGE OF HGK:

$$L_{HGK} = \{0, S, =, x, y, z, ..., f, g, h, ...\},$$

where $x, y, z, \ldots$ are integer variables, $f, g, h, \ldots$ function symbols, and S represents $x + 1$.

FORMATION RULES OF *HGK*. 1. A *numeral* is an expression on the form $0, S0, SS0, \ldots$ etc.

2. A *term* is defined by

1) 0 is a term.

2) Any variable is a term.

3) If t is a term, so is St.

4) If $t_1, \ldots, t_n$ are terms and f is an n-ary function symbols, then $f(t_1, \ldots, t_n)$ is a term.

3. An *equation* is an expression of the form $t = s$, where t and s are terms.

Let E be a finite set of equations. Then the members of E are axioms. An equation is a *derivation* from E if it can be obtained by repeated applications of the following rules of inference:

INFERENCE RULES OF *HGK*. 1. Given an equation we may replace all occurrences of a given variable x by a given numeral.

2. If $f(n_1, \ldots, n_k) = m$ is derivable, where m and n_i are numerals, then given an equation we may replace any occurrence

of $f(n_1,...,n_n)$ by m.

3. If $t = s$ is derived, then so is $s = t$.

DEFINITION. Let f be a k-ary function. Then

1. $f(x_1,...,x_k)$ is *defined* by HGK if and only if, for all $n_1,...,n_k$, there is a unique m such that,

$$[HGK \vdash f(n_1,...,n_k) = m] \leftrightarrow [f(x_1,...,x_k) = m].$$

2. f is *general recursive* (or simply *recursive*) if and only if it is defined by HGK.

By *Church's Thesis* that the class of effectively computable functions is the general recursive function, the notion of provability in HGK has been considered as the notion of *formal mathematical computation*.

2.2 Gödel's First Incompleteness Theorem

E. Post viewed the Gödel's incompleteness theorem as a fundamental discovery in the limitations of the mathematicizing powers of Homo Sapiens([Post 1936]). According to Post, Gödel's theorem concerning the incompleteness of first-order logic can be transformed into conclusions concerning all formal logics and all methods of solvability.

In 1931, Gödel proved that a formal system, in which all propositions of arithmetic can be expressed as meaningful formulas, is not complete. This means that Gödel established the incompleteness of a sufficiently strong axiomatic formal system. By introducing Gödel numbering of formal expressions, he arithmetized the syntax of primitive recursive extensions of the system *PM* from *Principia Mathematica* by B. Russell and A. Whitehead. Gödel then introduced a diagonal argument and constructed a Gödel sentence G, a formula with no free variables, that is not provable in *PM*.

Let T be a first-order formal theory that contains elementary arithmetic Z with the following axioms([Cohen 1966]): (Notation. $!\exists x A(x)$ as an abbreviation for $\exists x \forall y (A(y) \leftrightarrow x = y)$)

(Z1) $\forall x \forall y \exists !z (x + y = z)$

(Z2) $\forall x \forall y \exists !z (x \times y = z)$

(Z3) $\forall x (x + 0 = x) \wedge (x \times 1 = x)$

(Z4) $\forall x \forall y (x + (y + 1) = (x + y) + 1)$

(Z5) $\forall x \forall y (x \times (y + 1) = x \times y + 1)$

(Z6) $\forall x \forall y ((x + 1 = y + 1) \rightarrow (x = y)$

(Z7) $\forall x (\neg x + 1 = 0)$

(Z8) $\forall t_1, ..., t_k [(A_m(0, t_1, ..., t_k) \wedge \forall y (A_m(y, t_1, ..., t_k) \rightarrow$

$A_m(y + 1, t_1, ..., t_k))) \rightarrow \forall x A_m(x, t_1, ..., t_k)].$

(the principle of mathematical induction)

Let $\lceil A \rceil$, the code of A, be a term assigned to each formula A in T. Then we may define a substitution function sut such that for any formulas Ax, terms t with codes $\ulcorner t \urcorner$,

$$T \vdash sut(\ulcorner Ax \urcorner, \ulcorner t \urcorner) = \ulcorner At \urcorner.$$

PROVABILITY. Let $T \vdash A$ if and only if $T \vdash Pf_T(x,y)$ for some term t and

$$PROV_T(Y) \leftrightarrow \exists x Pf_T(x,y),$$

where $Pf_T(x,y)$ represents x *proves* y *in* T. Then there exists a provability predicate $PROV_T$ such that for any A in T,

$$(T \vdash A) \leftrightarrow (T \vdash PROV_T(\ulcorner A \urcorner)).$$

DIAGONALIZATION. Let Ax be a formula with one free variable. Then there is a statement B such that

$$T \vdash B \leftrightarrow A(\ulcorner B \urcorner).$$

Let $\theta x \leftrightarrow A(sut(x,x))$ be the diagonalization of A. Let $m = \ulcorner \theta x \urcorner$ and $B = \theta m$. Then

$$B \leftrightarrow \theta m$$
$$\leftrightarrow A(sut(m,m))$$
$$\leftrightarrow A(sut(\ulcorner \theta x \urcorner, m)$$
$$\leftrightarrow A(\ulcorner \theta m \urcorner)$$
$$\leftrightarrow A(\ulcorner B \urcorner).$$

THOEREM(Gödel's First Incompleteness Theorem). Let T be a consistent formal theory containing the arithmetic system Z, and

$$T \vdash G \leftrightarrow \neg PROV_T(\ulcorner G \urcorner).$$

Then neither $T \vdash G$ nor $T \vdash \neg G$.

By the diagonalization, we obtain a Gödel sentence G such that

$$T \vdash G \leftrightarrow \neg PROV_T(\ulcorner G \urcorner).$$

(i) If $T \vdash G \rightarrow T \vdash PROV_T(\ulcorner G \urcorner)$ by the provability, then $T \vdash \neg G$. This contradicts the consistency of T.

(ii) If $T \vdash \neg G \rightarrow T \vdash \neg PROV_T(\ulcorner \neg G \urcorner)$, then $T \vdash G$, by the provability condition. This contradicts the consistency of T.

THEOREM(Gödel's Second Incompleteness Theorem). Let T be a consistent formal theory containing the arithmetic system Z, and ($Cons(T)$ representing the consistency of T)

$$G \leftrightarrow Cons(T).$$

Then $Cons(T)$ is not provable in T.

Similarily, we say that a formal system S is *sound* for a formula Π_1^0 in S whenever Π_1^0 is true in the structure of natural numbers if S proves Π_1^0. It follows that a formal system S is consistent if and only if S is sound for Π_1^0. Here, we may consider Π_1^0 formulas as $\forall y D(x, y)$ with one free variable x and a decidable predicate D. In other words, the class of Π_1^0 formulas are ones of the form $\forall x D(x)$ representing for all variables x the predicate D holds, where the predicate D is a *decidable* property of natural numbers.

Let $PROV_S(x,y)$ be a decidable binary predicate expressing that y is a proof of the formula x in S. $PROV_S(x,y)$ is a decidable relation between two natural numbers x and y, that is, an algorithm exists to decide, for each choice of value of x and y, whether or not $PROV_S(x,y)$ holds. Then $\forall y \neg PROV_S(x,y)$ is in the class of Π_1^0 formulas. Gödel actually constructed a Π_1^0 sentence such as $G(S) \leftrightarrow \forall y \neg PROV_S(\gamma,y)$, where γ is the Gödel number of $G(S)$.

THEOREM(Gödel's First Incompleteness) If a formal system S is consistent then neither $G(S)$ nor $\neg G(S)$ is provable in S.

Let *MIND* be a mind that makes only true statements. Suppose that

$$G \leftrightarrow [\underline{MIND \text{ never proves } G \text{ is true}}].$$

Then [<u>*MIND* never proves G is true</u>] is false if *MIND* proves G is true. If [<u>*MIND* never proves G is true</u>] is false then G is false, since *MIND* never proves G is true. So if *MIND* proves that G is true, then G is false. Thus *MIND* makes a false statement. Thus *MIND* never proves that G is true, since *MIND* makes only true statements. Therefore,

[*MIND* never proves G is true] is a true statement. Hence, G is true by $G \leftrightarrow$ [*MIND* never proves G is true].

However, Gödel's metamathematical theorems are fundamentally different from so called Liar's paradoxes. Let α be the class of formulas that are not expressed in a system S, and β be the class of formulas that are expressed in S. Suppose $\beta \subseteq \alpha$, where β represents the class of formulas provable in S. Then Gödel proved that $\beta \subset \alpha$. By the soundness theorem, there exists a true sentence but not provable. Hence, Gödel's theorem is not a paradox([Gödel 1934]).

2.3 Gödel's Second Incompleteness Theorem

By formalizing the proof of the first incompleteness theorem, Gödel stated the second incompleteness theorem in his same work([Gödel 1931]).

THEOREM(Gödel's Second Incompleteness) If a formal system S is consistent then its own consistency, denoted by $Cons(S)$, is not provable in S.

In other words, let S be a formal system whose axioms are given by some recursive rule. If S is consistent and the primitive recursive functions can be embedded in S, then $Cons(S)$ cannot be proved in S.

The second incompleteness theorem may be restated from various perspectives. Versions of this theorem from Gödel's original to those of other scholars are as follows:

1. K. Gödel: *Let be any recursive consistent class of* FORMULAS; *then the* SENTENTIAL FORMULA *stating that is consistent is not* k-PROVABLE; in particular, the consistency of PM(Principia Mathematica) is not provable in PM, provided PM is consistent (in the opposite case, of course, every proposition is provable [in PM]) ([Gödel 1931, Theorem XI]).

2. S. Kleene: *If the number-theoretic formal system is (simply) consistent, then not prove* Cons; *i.e., if the system is consistent, then there is no consistency proof for it by methods formalizable in the system*([Kleene 1952, 210]).

3. P. Cohen: $Cons(Z_1)$ *cannot be proved in* Z_1 *(where* Z_1 *is the formal system for elementary arithmetic)*([Cohen 1966, 42]).

4. P. Smorynski: *Let* T *be a consistent formal theory containing arithmetic. Then* $Cons(T)$ *is not provable in* T ([Smorynski 1977, 825]).

5. T. Jech: *It is unprovable in set theory (unless it is inconsistent) that there exists a model of set theory*([Jech 1994, 311]).

6. R. Rucker: *If a formal system* T *satisfies conditions*

i) T is finitely given,

ii) T extends Principia Mathematica system P, and

iii) T is consistent,

then T does not prove $Cons(T)$ ([Rucker 1995, 291]).

7. S. Feferman: *If S is simply consistent then $Cons(S)$ is not provable in S* ([Feferman 1998, 62]).

8. H. DeLong: *No consistent human computer can prove his own consistency* ([DeLong 1970, 200]).

It is said that Gödel's incompleteness theorem was a fatal blow to the Hilbert's formalist program for the foundations of mathematics. Hilbert's idea of a proof theory, the formalization of mathematics and a finitist proof of consistency of mathematics is found in Hilbert [1927] ([Heijenoort 1967]).

Yet, this is not a trivially demonstrated statement. For Gödel himself did not deny the possibility of a finitist proof of the consistency of mathematics. As Gödel concluded:

The entire proof of Theorem XI [i.e., the Second Incompleteness Theorem] carries over word for word to the axiom system of set theory, $M,$ and to that of classical mathematics, A, and here, too, it yields the result: There is no consistency proof for M, or for A, that could be formalized in M, or A, respectively, provided M, or A is consistent.

I wish to note expressly that Theorem XI (and the corresponding results for M and A) do not contradict Hilbert's formalist viewpoint. For this viewpoint presupposes only the existence of a consistency proof in which nothing but finitary means of proof is used, and it is conceivable that there exist finitary proofs that *cannot* be expressed in the formalism of P [i.e., the formal system of Principia Mathematica] (or of M or A). (Italics in original, [Gödel 1931], 195).

According to Gödel, the second incompleteness theorem does not contradict Hilbert's formalist program, and there may be finitary proofs of $Cons(P)$ that cannot be representable in P. For, if we extend our system beyond a fixed system we can prove the consistency of various systems.

CHAPTER 3

Gödel and Symbolic Cognitive Science

3.1 Mapping from Mind to Machine

A physical symbol system is an instance of a Universal Turing machine. Thus, from a symbolic system we can deduce that cognition can be realized by a Universal Turing machine. Theoretically, the development of the first digital computer and of the automata theory originates in Turing's work [1936]. The chess programs of C. Shanon and A. Turing, LISP of J. McCarthy, Logic Theorist(LT) and General Problem Solver (GPS) of A. Newell, H. A. Simon and J. C. Shaw, PROLOG of F. Green, R. Kowalski and A. Colmerauer, SOAR of A. Newell, J. Laird, and P. Rosenbloom, Automated Mathematician program of R. Davis and D. B. Lenat, and Boyer-Moore theorem prover of R. S. Boyer and J. S. Moore are just some of the significant theoretical and historical works worth noting.

Since Turing's abstract device is regarded as the embodiment of a method of mathematical thinking at the most fundamental level, then the computer and cognitive scientists' claim on the Turing machine as a conceptual tool is now at least as strong as the logician's one. Its significance for the computability theory is fundamental: within a finite time, the Turing machine is capable of any computation that can be done by any modern digital computer, no matter how powerful. We cannot get away from the Turing machine if we want that computation by the current computer to happen. Thus, for the theoretical study of the ultimate problem-solving capacity of the real computer, the Turing machine and its degree is a necessary condition.

Turing's analysis transformed the term *finite procedure* into *mechanical procedure*. Consequently, a function is computable, or effectively calculable, if it can be calculated by a finite mechanical procedure, that is, by a Turing machine. Gödel claimed that a formal system can simply be defined as any mechanical procedure for producing formulas, called provable formulas([Gödel 1964]). In this sense, a function is Turing computable if it is definable by a Turing machine([Turing 1936]). According to this framework, a formal mind as a Turing machine yields m on input n if, when the machine is started on input n, it eventually halts, and at the moment when it halts, the tape represents m.

3.2 Turing Machines

The Turing machine is a finite automaton with unlimited tape as a memory device. It is mathematically equivalent to the class of the Herbrand-Gödel-Kleene equation system, that is the class of general recursive functions([Gödel 1934, Kleene 1952]).

Rather, Gödel endorsed the concept of Turing machines as a generally accepted property of effective calculability, not as general recursion defined by himself. Turing devised an idealized human computing agent with the concepts of function produced by mechanical procedure([Gödel 1946, 1951, 1963]).

Turing's theorem [1936] states that any function calculable by an idealized human computer is Turing computable. Furthermore, Turing's thesis asserts that if a function is informally computable, then it is computed by a Turing idealized human computer, meaning that every algorithm can be programmed on a one-tape Turing machine.

A Turing machine is characterized by the following(figure 3):

1. A list of states called by Turing machine configurations:

a specification of how many states there are.

2. A finite alphabet of symbols, including blank and stroke.

3. A finite set of lists of instructions. Each instruction has the form of the quintuple

$$(i,s,t,\Phi,j),$$

where i and j are numbers no greater than the number of states, s and t are elements of the alphabet, and Φ is either R(move one right) or L(move one left). The instructions may be read: if in state i and scanning a cell containing s, then replace s with t, move as Φ directs, and go into new state j.

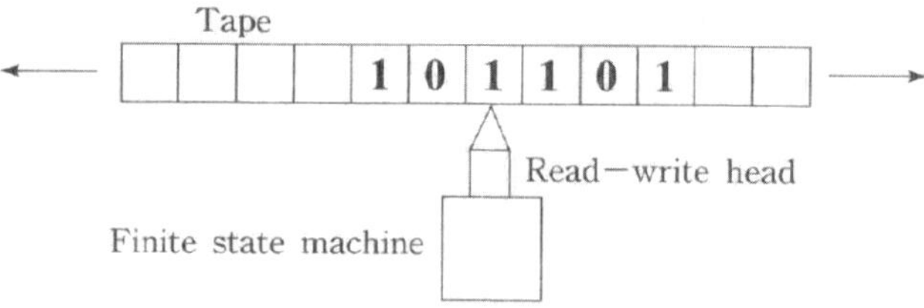

Figure 3. Turing Machine

DEFINITION. Let S be a finite set of symbols including Blank 0 and Stroke 1, and let $q_1, q_2, .., q_n$ $(n \in N)$ be symbols of states not in S. Then a Turing machine on S is a finite set of quintuples

$$(q_i, s, t, \Phi, q_j),$$

where s and t are in S and Φ is one of the symbols R(move one right) or L(move one left), such that no two distinct quintuples have the same first two members. The symbol q_i represents the state i. Mathematically, a Turing machine is a mapping TM such that for some natural number n,

$$TM: \{0,1,2,...,n\} \times \{0,1\} \to \{0,1\} \times \{L, R\} \times \{0,1,2,...,n\}$$

where L stands for move one left and R move one right(figure 2).

For example, if

$$TM_{x+y} = \left\{ \begin{array}{l} (q_1,1,1,R,q_1),(q_1,0,1,R,q_2),(q_2,1,1,R,q_2), \\ (q_2,0,1,L,q_3),(q_3,1,0,L,q_4),(q_4,1,0,L,q_5), \\ (q_5,1,0,L,q_6),(q_6,1,1,L,q_6),(q_6,0,0,R,q_0) \end{array} \right\},$$

then TM_{x+y} computes addition $x+y$:

$(q_1,1,1,R,q_1)$: pass over x

$(q_1,0,1,R,q_2)$: full gap

$(q_2,1,1,R,q_2)$: pass over y

$(q_2,0,1,L,q_3)$: end of y

$(q_3,1,0,L,q_4)$: erase 1

$(q_4,1,0,L,q_5)$: erase 1

$(q_5,1,0,L,q_6)$: erase 1

$(q_6,1,1,L,q_6)$: back up

$(q_6, 0, 0, R, q_0)$: halt.

Physically, a course of process can only consist of the following three steps:

1. A symbol is written on the tape square being scanned, thereby erasing the previous symbol.
2. The Turing machine moves one square to the right or left.
3. The next state is specified.

Turing [1936] compared a man in the process of computing a real number to a machine that is only capable of a finite number of conditions that is called *m-configurations*. According to Turing, the behavior of the machine is determined by the *m-configuration* q_n and the scanned symbol s_r. This pair (q_n, s_r) is called the *configuration*. Thus, the configuration determines the possible behavior of the machine. Since there are only finitely many pairs, the behavior of the machine is specified by a finite list.

UNIVERSAL TURING MACHINE([Turing 1936]). For a recursive function F, there exists a universal Turing machine UTM such that

$$F_{TM_n}(x) = F_{UTM}(n, x)$$

for any Turing machine TM_n and for any natural numbers n and x. This is to say that there is a universal Turing machine that can simulate any Turing machine.

3.3 The Computability of Turing Machine

A. Turing proved that Hilbert's 10th problem, *Endscheidungsproblem*,(decision problem), of discovering a method for establishing the truth or falsity of any statement in first-order logic, was impossible to solve by the Turing machine([Turing 1936]). As Gödel stated,

In consequence of later advances, in particular of the fact that, due to A. M. Turing's work, a precise and unquestionably adequate definition of the general concept of formal system can now be given, the existence of undecidable arithmetical propositions and the non-demonstrability of the consistency of a system in the same system can now be proved rigorously for *every* consistent formal system containing a certain amount of finitary number theory. ([Gödel 1964])

DEFINITION([Turing 1936]). A sequence is said to be computable if it can be computed by a Turing machine. A number is computable if it differs by an integer from the number computed by a Turing machine.

A function f is *Turing computable* if there exists a Turing machine *TM* that computes f. For an n-place function f, *TM* computes f if and only if, any $x_1,...,x_n$ of the natural numbers, *TM* produces $f(x_1,...,x_n)$ on input x. It is well known that Turing computable function f is a decidable $(n+1)$-ary relation and a recursively enumerable relation. A set A is recursively *enumerable* if A is empty set or is the range of a general recursive function.

G. Chaitin deals with the halting problem in terms of Gödel's work([Chaitin 1995]). He shows that a halting probability number is expressed by $\Omega = \sum_{p\,halts} 2^{-|p|}$, which is an extreme case where reasoning fails completely. Chaitin then asserts that the halting probability is algorithmically irreducible or algorithmically random. Whether the halting problem is unsolvable by a Turing machine is a question concerning Turing machines themselves, prompting a metamathematical rather than a mathematical question. The halting function for the Turing machine is a mechanical implementation of Gödel's undecidable sentences. Gödel [1964] stated that Turing's 1936 paper provides an adequate analysis of mechanical procedures and that, as a consequence of his work, a general formulation of the incompleteness theorems can be given.

Turing himself demonstrated the limitations of Turing computability, proving that there are unsolvable problems, e.g., the

Halting Problem, in the Turing machine system.

LIMITATION OF TURING MACHINE. There is no Turing machine TM such that, for all e and n, if the Turing machine Gödel-numbered e produces something on input n then TM produces 0 on input (e,n); if the Turing machine Gödel-numbered e produces nothing on input n then TM produces 1 on input (e,n)([Turing 1936], 132-134).

For example, let $K = \{x : \varphi_x(x)\,halts\}$, where φ_e is partial recursive function computed by a Turing machine program with Gödel number e. Then the set K is recursively enumerable, but not recursive([Soare 1987]).

This result known as the effective unsolvability of the Halting problem for the Turing machines represents an upper bound to the set of computable functions by programs for current digital computers. This is equivalent to Church's theorem that the decision problem for first-order calculus is not solvable. Thus, the results show that Hilbert's Entscheidungsproblem can not be solved. As Turing stated that,

For each of these "general process" problems can be expressed as a problem concerning a general process for determining whether a given integer n has a property $G(n)$(e.g. $G(n)$ might mean "n is satisfactory" or "n is the Gödel representation of a provable formula"), and this is equivalent to computing a number whose

n-th figure 1 if $G(n)$ is true and 0 if it is false([Turing 1936], 134).

Gödel showed that there are undecidable propositions and that no proof of the consistency of *Principia Mathematica* can be given within the formal system. Turing as well states that,

> I shall show that there is no general method which tells whether a given formula U is provable in Principia Mathematica, or what comes to the same, whether the system consisting of Principia Mathematica with $\neg U$ adjoined as an extra axiom is consistent ([Turing 1936], 145).

Both Gödel's and Turing's theorems show the limitations of the first-order calculus system or of recursive universal machines. From this point of view, Turing machines can compute only a proper subset of the functions. Thus, if the mind is a Turing machine and cognition is a Turing computable function, then the mind would not be able to compute such Halting functions, because they would not be in the class of cognition.

LIMITATION OF COGNITION AS TURING COMPUTABLE FUNCTION. Let cognition COG be a Turing computable function. Then there is non-computable cognition on the natural numbers. We want to show that there exists a non-computable function in Turing computable functions over the natural numbers. Suppose that all Turing computable functions are computable. Then there are a countable number of Turing computable functions $COG: \mathbb{N} \to \mathbb{N}$.

Enumerate the functions $COG_1, COG_2, \dots$. And define a Turing computable function $COG: \mathbb{N} \to \mathbb{N}$ by

$$COG(x) = COG_x(x) + 1.$$

Since COG is a Turing computable function, it must appear somewhere in our list of computable functions.

Put $COG = COG_k$. But then

$$COG_k(k) = COG(k) = COG_k(k) + 1,$$

which is a contradiction. Thus, the function COG is not computable.

3.4 Gödel's Objection to Turing's Mechanism

Turing claimed that it is possible to construct a machine to do the work of the human as a computer([Turing 1936]). According to Turing, to each state of mind of the human computer corresponds an m-configuration of the Turing machine. As Turing asserted:

The behaviour of the computer [the human computer] at any moment determined by the symbols which he is observing, and his state of mind at that moment. We may suppose that there is a bound B to the number of symbols or squares which the computer can observe at one moment. If he wishes to that the number of states of mind which need be taken into account is finite. The reason for this are of the same character as those which restrict the number of symbols. If we admitted an infinity of states of mind, some of them will be arbitrarily close and will be confused. Again, the restriction is not one which seriously affects computation, since the use of more complicated states of mind can be avoided by writing more symbols on the tape([Turing 1936], 136).

His idea is based on that the simple operations of the Turing machine must include:

(a) Changes of the symbol on one of the observed squares.

(b) Changes of one of the squares observed to another square within squares of one of the previously observed squares.

Turing told:

It may be that some of these changes necessarily involve a change of state of mind. The most general single operation must therefore be taken to be one of the following:

(A) A possible change (a) of symbol together with a possible change of state of mind.

(B) A possible change (b) of observed squares, together with a possible change of state of mind([Turing 1936], 137).

Gödel interpreted Turing's argument as meaning that mental procedures cannot go beyond mechanical procedures([Gödel 1972]). Although Gödel accepted Turing's analysis of the computability, he did not agree with Turing on this point. Gödel pointed out that Turing's argument is inconclusive:

What Turing disregards completely is the fact that *mind, in its use, is not static, but constantly developing*, i.e., that we understand abstract terms more and more precisely as we go on using them, and that more and more abstract terms enter the sphere of our understanding(Italics in original, [Gödel 1972], 306).

In Gödel's view, Turing disregarded temporal elements of the mental capability. In contrast, he avoided the term *static*. Rather, Gödel himself focused on the developing process as a significant capability of cognition. Consequently, Gödel [1972] suggested two possibilities such as existence and convergence:

1. There may exist systematic methods of actualizing this development;

2. Turing's number of *distinguishable states of mind* may *converge toward infinity.*

This process refers to forming of stronger and stronger axioms of infinity in set theory. According to Gödel's account, such developing processes would produce a non-recursive number-theoretic function.

The existence of *finite non-mechanical procedures* is not excluded by Turing's analysis. Gödel claimed:

[T]he question of whether there exist finite *non-mechanical* procedures, not equivalent with any algorithm, has nothing whatsoever to do with the adequacy of the definition of formal system and of mechanical procedure(Italics in original, [Gödel 1964], 370).

According to Gödel's interpretation, the existence of mechanical procedures is required by the concept of formal system that cognition can be completely replaced by mechanical operations on formulas.

Gödel claimed that the incompleteness results do not limit the powers of human reason([Gödel 1964]).

Note that the results mentioned in this postscript do not

establish any bounds for the powers of human reason, but rather than for the potentialities of pure formalism in mathematics([Gödel 1964], 370).

Gödel chose a positive way to the higher posers of human cognition against Turing's mechanism. His objection is consistent with his disjunctive conclusion(see Chapter V).

3.5 Turing Machine Beyond Gödel's Incompleteness

To overcome the computational limitation of the Turing machine, Turing proposed an extension of his machine model([Turing 1939]). This idea gave rise to important issues such as *arithmetical hierarchy* and *relative recursiveness*([Soare 1987; Enderton 1977; Davis 1958]).

ORACLE TURING MACHINE. An *oracle Turing machine* is simply a Turing machine with an extra "read only" tape, called the *oracle tape*, upon which is written the characteristic function of some set O called the *oracle*, and whose symbols cannot be printed over. The old tape is called the *work tape*. The reading head moves along both tapes simultaneously.

An Oracle Turing machine is a function OTM such that for some natural number n,

$$OTM: \{0,1,2,...,n\} \times \{0,1,2\} \times \{0,1\} \rightarrow$$

$$\{0,1\} \times \{L, R\} \times \{0,1,2,...,n\}$$

where $\{0,1,2\}$ is the oracle tape alphabet, L stands for "move one left" and R for "move one right".

An oracle O for a function $f: N \rightarrow N$ is a device that, for a natural number $n \in N$, responds the value $f(n)$. Suppose A and B are arbitrary sets, and for all $n \in N$,

$$n \in A \ \leftrightarrow \ f(n) \in B.$$

Then, we have a decision procedure for membership in A if we have a decision procedure for membership in B. If there exists a decision procedure which computes $f(n)$ from n using an oracle O for B, for all $n \in N$, then A is reducible to B through f, written $A \leq_f B$. The oracle tape, therefore, is a query tape. An oracle O for B is an external agent that will supply the correct answer to questions of the form "$x \in B$" or not, for every $x \in N$. We can replace f by a Turing machine if f is recursive. By this, we can consider the problem of relative computability or relative reducibility.

Although the oracle has a new and powerful feature, it is the least constructive approach. It is remarkable to note that

1. O is not necessarily identified with an algorithm,

2. B may not be recursive,

3. f may accept members of N as arguments.

The oracle model is clearly more powerful than Turing machine, but it is also clear that the power comes from the addition of a function that was previously not computable. This leads to a recursive function that accepts members of the uncountable set as inputs, which raises the problem of relative computations on recursive infinite functions.

The extension model, however, still cannot give us any real idea of how to compute the halting function([Parberry 1994]). Moreover, such an infinite machine is beyond the scope of our debate, for it does not satisfy the assumptions underlying the finite machine, the type specified, or the consistency condition.

In Turing's view, for a given formal system TM_1, one can add the statement $Cons(TM_1)$ of consistency of TM_1 as a new axiom to TM_1 in order to obtain TM_2. Similarly we can obtain $Cons(TM_2)$, $Cons(TM_3)$,.... Turing's findings imply that any true sentence is provable at some state in the transfinite iteration process. This process is clearly not complete within some finitary means. For example, in 1935, G. Gentzen already established the proof of the consistency of formalized arithmetic by intuitive use of transfinite induction as far as the countable ordinal. Consequently, it is totally dependent on the assumption and philosophy of logicians. Thus, this is an act of faith and lies outside our discussion.

CHAPTER 4

Gödel and Connectionist Cognitive Science

It has been carelessly argued by many scholars that the human mind is superior to the computing machine just in terms of Turing machines. While Turing attempted to give a formal reduction of cognition in Turing machine models, McCulloch and Pitts tried to provide a formal reduction in their neural network model. Even though the computability of brain model is too significant to overlook, scholarly debate has neglected the cognitive computability of neural networks. Our present goal is to show that implications of neural computability for the mind brain and machine controversy.

In this chapter, we discover the computability of neural networks in terms of Gödel incompleteness theorems. Next we discuss the significance of neural computability. The term neural networks used here refers to cognitive systems obtained from a finite number of neurons by means of weighted interconnections. The implication of Gödel's incompleteness theorems for neural networks will provide a new perspective in understanding cognition as a meta-cognition, and not as a Turing machine computation. Throughout this chapter, we assume neural networks as an idealized mathematical model of the brain.

4.1 Mapping from Mind to Brain

The term *neural network* may refer to the circuitry of a real brain. By a neural network, we mean here a formal model of the brain, that is, an artificial neural network, rather than an actual brain. Developing a Turing computation model could provide insights into the processing of information in a brain-like computing machine.

In their paper [McCulloch and Pitts 1943], Warren McCulloch and Walter Pitts first formulated a mathematical model of structures and functions of the brain. With a formal model of the neuron as a threshold logic unit. They, in principle, provided the *physiology of the computable*, showing that each Turing machine program could be implemented, using a finite network of their formal neurons. Their goal was to replace *from computing machine to cognition* with *from com-*

puting brain to cognition. Thus, the formal neuron models developed by McCulloch and Pitts were primarily designed as a system for an analysis of the logic of the nervous system rather than for an accurate neurophysiological description. Although the real biological neuron is much more complex, their models suffice for representing formal aspects of brain functioning.

The use of a brain-style computational system offer two advantages([Rumelhart 1989; Arbib 1995]):

1. An understanding of how brains work,
2. A solution to computational problems that seem difficult to achieve in Turing machine frameworks.

The study of neural networks has been interdisciplinary from the fields of neurobiology, psychology, computer science, and physics([Widrow & Lehr 1990]). The development of mathematical models for neural computing began more than fifty years ago with the computing machine model by McCulloch & Pitts [1943], the *learning and adaptation* model by Hebb [1949], the *learning from experience* model by Rosenblatt [1959], the *backpropagation* model by Rumelhart, Hinton, and Williams [1986] and others([Amari [1990]). This work of modeling the brain has succeeded in solving important problems encountered in pattern recognition and optimization.

However, the different properties of the neural network

model pay little attention to the study of neural networks in terms of Turing computability. The term *connectionism* is here used in reference to studies on human mathematical thinking in terms of the parallel distributed network model, that is, a neural network. For example, Marvin Minsky asserts that minds are simply what brains do([Minsky 1985]). My assumption, however, does not necessarily mean that the mind is just a subset of functions of the brain. A neural network is said to be a collection of connected elements or units.

4.2 Neural Networks

In his paper([Kohonen 1988]), T. Kohonen introduced the following definition:

Artificial neural networks are massively parallel interconnected networks of simple(usually adaptive) elements and their hierarchical organizations which are intended to interact with the objects of the real world in the same way as biological nervous systems do(Italics in original, [Kohonen 1988], 4).

This definition represents motives of neural computing. From a formal perspective, we will investigate more detailed notions and original ideas of neural network.

Unifying the studies of neurophysiology and mathematical logic, W. McCulloch and W. Pitts [1943] formulated a formal neuron model as a threshold unit that could act as a control device for any Turing machine. McCulloch and Pitts offered a brain model of the computable, whereas Turing offered a mind model of the computable. Under the assumptions of McCulloch and Pitts, a *neuron* consists of a *soma*, where axons lead to one or more *endbulbs*.

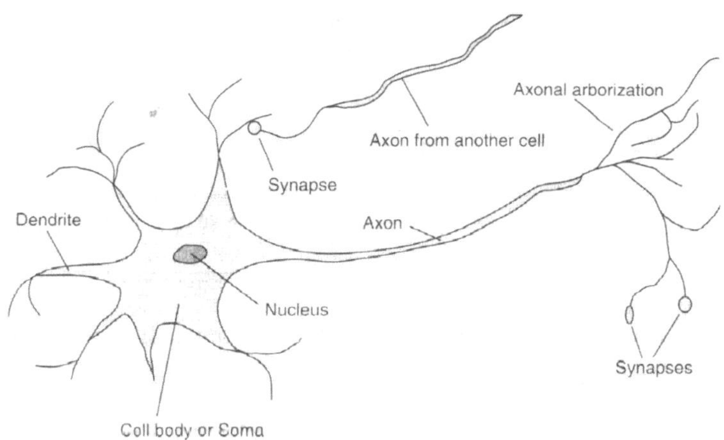

Fingure 4. Neuron

DEFINITION([Kleene 1952]). A *neural network* is an arrangement of a finite number of neurons in which each endbulb of any neuron is adjacent to(impinges on) the soma of not more than one neuron(the same or another); the separating gap is a *synapse*. Each endbulb is either *excitatory* or *inhibitory*(not both). We call the neurons(zero or more) on which no endbulbs impinge *input neurons*; the others, *inner neurons*(figure 4).

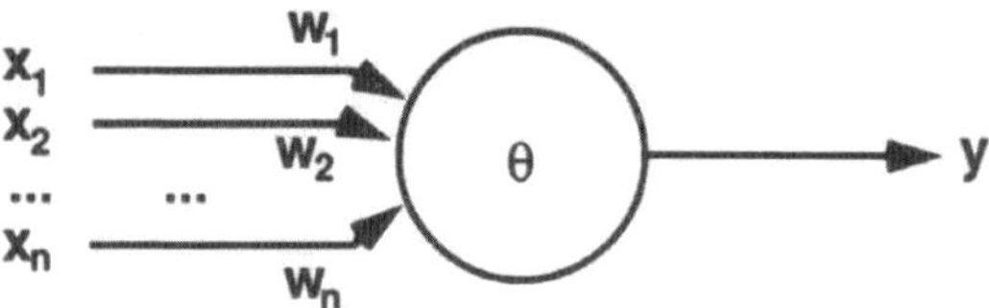

Figure 5. Formal Neuron

DEFINITION. A *McCulloch-Pitts neuron*(or *threshold logic unit*) is an element with, say, n inputs $x_1,...,x_n (n \geq 1)$ and the output y. It is characterized by $n+1$ numbers, its threshold θ, and the weights $w_1,...,w_n$, where w_i is associated with x_i (figure 5). Taking a refractory period as the unit of time, we postulate that the neuron operates on a time scale $t = 1,2,...$, the firing of its output at time $t+1$ if the weighted sum of its inputs at time t exceeds the threshold of the neuron, which rule may be expressed symbolically as

$$y(t+1) \leftrightarrow \sum_i w_i x_i(t) \geq \theta.$$

DEFINITION. A *neural network* is a collection of McCulloch-Pitts neurons, each with the same time scale, interconnected by splitting the output of any neuron into a number of lines and connecting some or all of these to the inputs of other neurons. An output may thus lead to any number of inputs, but an input may come from at most one output([Arbib 1987]).

According to this definition, a neural network can be viewed as a discrete-time dynamical system. Such a network functions like a finite automaton whose state, given by the firing pattern of all the constituent neurons, changes synchronously on a time scale.

McCulloch and Pitts asserted that the control mechanism of the universal Turing machine could be simulated by a finite set of formalized neurons connected to each other by synapses. The *McCulloch-Pitts neuron* is a binary device. It can be in only two possible states. Each neuron has a fixed threshold. The neuron can receive inputs from excitatory synapses, all of which have identical weights. If inhibitory synapses are active, the neuron cannot fire. There is a time quantum for integration of synaptic inputs, based loosely on the physiologically observed delay.

The mode of operation of the McCulloch-Pitts neuron is very simple. During the time quantum, the neuron responds to the activity of its synapses, which reflect the state of the presynaptic cells. If no inhibitory synapses are active, the neuron adds its synaptic inputs and checks to see if the sum meets or exceeds its threshold. If it does, then the neuron fires and is active. If it does not, the neuron is inactive.

McCulloch and Pitts showed that neural events and the relations between them could be treated by means of Boolean logic because of the *all-or-none* character of nerve activity. Each neuron is a finite-state machine and hence operates in discrete time. The formal results concerning networks of logical elements also were used in von Neumann. Although their simplified model is sufficient for certain discussions, it should be noted that more realistic models of the brain differ from the models of the McCulloch-Pitts neuron in two ways([Arbib 1987], 21).

DEFINITION. Let NN be a neural network. Then NN is regarded as an arbitrarily (I) *directed* or *undirected*, and (II) *cyclic* or *acyclic* graph of a function. If the nodes as formal neurons are finitely numbered, then NN is finite; otherwise, NN is infinite.

Like Turing machines, the language of finite neural networks consists of finite alphabets, and its inference rule has certain activation rules, such that

$$y(t+1) \ \leftrightarrow \ \sum_i w_i x_i(t) \geq \theta \ (i = 1,2,...).$$

where x is inputs, y the output, $t = 1,2,...$ time scale, θ

threshold, and w weights(for more on the activation rules, see [Williams, 1986]).

DEFINITION([Garzon 1995]). A discrete neural network is a triple $NN= <A, D, \{f_i\}>$ consisting of a set with an additive-multiplicative structure A, a countable(finite or infinite), locally-finite, arc-weighted, digraph D, and a family of activation functions f_i, one for each vertex i in D. The local dynamics of NN is defined by equations:

$$net_i(t+1) = \sum_j w_{ij} a_j(t)$$

where the sum is taken over all cells j supporting links into i, and

$$a_j(t) = f_j(net_j(t))$$

is the activation of the cell j at time t.

Moreover, if $x_j(t)$ is the state of neuron j at time t, taking values in the set of natural numbers, f_j the neuron activation function, I_j the external input of neuron j, and w_{ij} are the connection weights from neuron i to neuron j. Then a discrete-time neural network is

$$x_j(t+1) = f\left(\sum_{i=1}^{n} w_{ij} x_i(t) + I_j\right).$$

In all, the neural network NN is a quintuple (V, X, Y, E, a), where V is a finite set of nodes, $X \cap V = \varnothing$ is a set of inputs, $Y \subseteq V$ is a set of outputs, $E = V \times V$ is a connection, $(V \cup X, E)$ is a directed (undirected) weighted graph, and $a: V \rightarrow F$ is a node assignment function (F is the set of node functions). The primitive functions computed in the formal neuron can be selected arbitrarily. Thus, Fourier series and fuzzy logic can be implemented as a neural network. We, however, need a kind of axiom that there is a choice function.

DEFINITION. The connection is defined by a 2-tuple (E, W), where W is a set of weights. Hence, NN can be essentially characterized by the function

$$NN: X \times W \times \{\theta\} \rightarrow Y.$$

There are different types of connections: (1) fully or partially connected; (2) feed-forward or feed-back connected; (3) bi-directional or directional connected; (4) hierarchical or non-hierarchical connected; and (5) resonance.

For example, the ART(Adaptive Resonance Theory) models of neural networks have three layers: the input layer is fully connected to the next layer in a hierarchical connected; the other two layers have a resonance connection([Carpenter and Grossberg 1995]).

A *configuration* of NN is a list of finite activation functions that correspond one to one with the set of nodes V. The number of nodes in a directed graph is its *order*, and the number of links, that is, connections, is its *size*. Thus, *NN* is a structure of neurons and connections, where neuron is a state and connection is an operation. *NN* defined here as a connectionist and parallel distributed system requires that neurons communicate their state changes to all others synchronously.

Models of Neural Networks

Athough there are many kinds of neural networks, neural network theory can be said to be currently dominated by two basic models; the McCulloch-Pitts neuron and its variants, and the leaky integrator neuron([Arbib 1995]). The former refers to neural networks in discrete time-space, whereas the latter refers to neural networks in continuous time-space. Both models were developed by finding a proper activation function and a learning rule.

Lippmann introduced six important neural networks by classifying them as either binary and continuous-valued inputs, or as supervised and unsupervised training styles([Lippmann 1987]). According to his classifications, these six networks may be characterized as follows:

1. Hopfield Network: binary-valued input, supervised training.

2. Hamming Network: binary-valued input, supervised train-

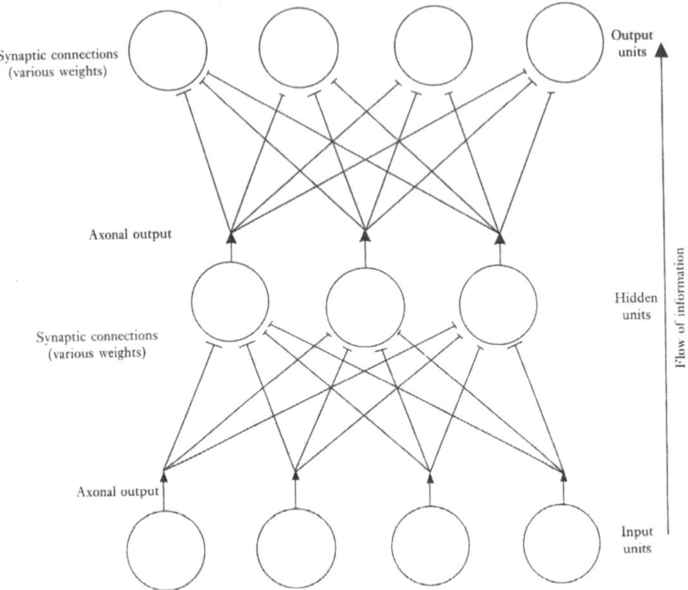

Figure 6. A Simple Neural Network

ing, optimum classifier.

3. Carpenter & Grossberg Classifier: binary-valued input, unsupervised training, leader clustering algorithm.

4. Perceptron: continuous-valued input, supervised training, Gaussian classifier.

5. Multi-Layer Perceptron: continuous-valued input, unsupervised training, -nearest neighbor mixture.

6. Kohonen Self-Organizing Feature Maps: continuous-valued input, unsupervised training, -means clustering

algorithm.

For a more effective discussion, we could employ just two classification dimensions, such as finite/infinite and feed-forward/recurrent. Both *finite* and *infinite* neural networks may be further classified into two models.

Finite and Infinite Neural Networks

FINITE NEURAL NETWORKS. A finite neural network is a formal neural network with finite neurons([Cosnard 1995]).

1. Threshold Network: discrete neural networks.

2. PRAM(Parallel Random Access Machine): uniform family of Boolean Circuit.

INFINITE NEURAL NETWORKS. A infinite neural network is a formal neural network with infinite neurons([Cosnard 1995]).

1. Cellular Automata: infinite memory, homogeneous functions, all cells and finite automata.

2. Infinite Neural Network: arbitrary graph, computing with real numbers.

Feed-forward and Recurrent Neural Networks

Feed-forward (*recurrent*) neural networks are also characterized by two models.

FEED-FORWARD NETWORKS. A *feed-forward* or *non-recurrent* neural network is a neural network with a directed graph $(V \cup X, E)$. A classical neural network MP (McCulloch-Pitts Network) can be specified as a feed-forward neural network with a *Boolean linear threshold function* $b : \{0,1\}^n \rightarrow \{0,1\}$, for some natural number n.

RECURRENT NETWORKS. A *recurrent* or *feedback* neural network is a neural network with a graph $(V \cup X, E)$. It is well known that recurrent networks can simulate finite state automata([Cleermans, Servan-Schreiber & McClelland 1989]).

A *Backpropagation network* is a recurrent neural network with a *sigmoidal function*

$$s : \mathbb{R}^n \rightarrow [0,1]$$

that is a weighted threshold function, such that for any $X \in \mathbb{R}^n$,

$$s(X) = \frac{1}{1+e^{-x}}$$

where $X = \sum_{i=1}^{n} w_i x_i$ with for any real number $x \in \mathbb{R}$, and for some real weights $w \in \mathbb{R}$. In many current studies, it is customary to use the sigmoid function or, equivalently, the hyperbolic tangent $\tanh(x)$.

EXAMPLES. 1. McCulloch-Pitts Network NN_{MP} is generally characterized by the following properties:

1) feed-forward network,

2) nondifferentiable network,

3) nonlinear network(referred to as *linear threshold* by [Minsky & Papert 1988]),

4) finite state network,

5) single-layer network.

Thus, NN_{MP} has linear separability and hence NN_{MP} cannot compute the parity function (or XOR function) $\oplus : \{0,1\}^n \rightarrow \{0,1\}$ such that

$\forall x, y \in \{0,1\}$, $x \oplus y = 1$ if and only if $(x = 1) \vee (y = 1)$ but $x \neq y$.

Perceptron, an extension of McCulloch-Pitts neural network, also does not have linear separability.

EXAMPLE. 2. Hopfield Network([Hopfield 1982]) is generally characterized by the following properties:

1) recurrent network,

2) differentiable network,

3) nonlinear network,

4) infinite state network,

5) symmetric network, i.e., undirectional network,

6) multi-layered network.

In a Hopfield network, each neuron is updated by computing a threshold function $f : \mathbb{R}^n \to \{1, -1\}$ of the current states of the other neurons. Hopfield network is said to be an *associative memory* system if there is a set of n patterns $P = \{x_1, ..., x_n\}$ such that when a new input pattern $\bar{x}$ is presented as the input, the associative memory outputs a pattern $x_k \in P$ that is closest to $\bar{x}$ among all the patterns in P.

If a pattern $\bar{x}$ is applied to Hopfield network as the initial state, Hopfield network converges to a stable state in P that is closest to $\bar{x}$. Hopfield network has the *updating rule*([Hopfield 1982]): Pick a unit at random. If the sum of the weights on connections to other active units is positive, turn it on. Otherwise, turn it off.

4.3 The Computability of Neural Network

A new connectionist approach arose in the 1980s, that combined the insights of the studies on *learning networks* in the 1950s and 1960s with subsequent theoretical refinements, such as *backpropagation algorithm,* that grew from more than two decades of studies in AI. Thus, connectionism has built new computational models of cognition in the form of parallel network systems. The basic idea of the connectionist approach is to consider an abstract neuron as its fundamental processing unit.

A connectionist neural network model is used both to model mental processes and to simulate actual behavior. In contrast with Turing machine models, a neural network model focuses on a highly adaptive system by adjusting its weights, not by conventional programming. Indeed it has an essentially different representational property from the compositionality and systematicity of symbolic representation. Neural network studies have the following important characteristics([Arbib 1987]):

1. Ability to bring multiple interacting constraints to bear on problem-solving.

2. Associative and content-addressable memory.

3. Generalization: adaptability in parametrized systems in which the topology of parameter space can be linked to the similarity

of the functions that the networks are to serve.

4. Rules as emergent properties rather than explicit symbolic structures.

5. Speed of processing from exploitation of parallelism.

Connectionism, therefore, is not merely synonymous with use of distributed computation in computer science.

D. E. Rumelhart, G. H. Hinton and J. L. McClelland [1986] formulated the following eight major aspects of a Parallel Distributed Processing model:

1. A set of processing units.

2. A state of activation defined over the processing units.

3. An output function for each unit that maps its state of activation into an output.

4. A pattern of connectivity among units.

5. A propagation rule for propagating patterns of activities through the network of connectivities.

6. An activation rule for combining the inputs impinging on a unit with the current state of that unit to produce a new level of activation for the unit.

7. A learning rule whereby patterns of connectivity are modified by experience.

8. An environment within which the system must operate.

D. E. Rumelhart [1989] listed seven major components of any connectionist system without stating a propagation rule. According to Rumelhart, in a system of neural networks, short-term storage can occur in the states of units, long-term storage can take place in the connections between units. Knowledge is, therefore, *implicit* in the networks as a whole rather than explicit in the state of units. This knowledge then is acquired through connections of units rather than formulated as a declarative statement.

Here, *activation rule*, *learning rule* and *environment* are part of the computational and representational functions of the neurons. There are three basic kinds of modifications of the patterns of interconnectivity involved in changing the processing or knowledge structure in a neural network model:

1. The development of new connections.
2. The loss of existing connections.
3. The modification of the strengths of connections that already exist.

According to Bechtel and Abrahamsen [1991], the above seven properties used to distinguish the different types of connectionist architectures can actually be reduced to four:

1. The connectivity of units.

2. The activation function of units.

3. The nature of the learning procedure that modifies the connections between units.

4. How the network is interpreted semantically.

LEARNING. One of the most significant characteristics of neural networks may be the *adaptivity* that comes from their learning capability([Rumelhart 1989]). According to D. Waltz [1988], neural networks show three important abilities: (1) learning, (2) associative recall, and (3) fault tolerance([Vapnik 1995]).

Learning in neural networks is based on changing the weights on links, whereas learning in Turing machines is based on the rule. The neural network itself can generate new weights, but the Turing machine itself cannot generate new rules. Consequently, learning in neural networks takes place within that system, whereas learning in Turing machines usually takes place outside the system. On this point, learning in Turing machine systems is external to the system. On the other hand, learning in neural network systems is internal to the system.

In Turing machines, the knowledge is obtained outside the system, and then coded into the data base. On the other hand, in neural networks, the knowledge is stored as the strength of connections among neurons. In this sense, the neural network is a learning system that changes itself. Neural network systems learn from examples, and infer a general procedure for classifying future examples. Thus, learning by neural networks is inductive rather than deductive.

EXAMPLE. A classical learning rule is the Widrow-Hoff rule, known as the *Delta Rule*, which is formulated as

$$r_i = z[(t) - y(t)]x_i(t)$$

where t is the target pattern, $y(t)$ the network's output, and $x_i(t)$ the input to the network. Since this rule is dependent on an external teacher, it is classified as *supervised learning*.

The *Generalized Delta Rule* is a generalization of the Widrow-Hoff delta rule for training *Adaline*(ADAptive LInear Neuron) network. *Backpropagation* in principle comes from the Generalized Delta Rule(a more technical statement is found in[Widrow & Lehr 1995]). According to Werbos [1995], backpropagation has two standard definitions:

1. Backpropagation is a procedure for *efficiently* calculating the derivatives of some output quantities of a nonlinear system, with respect to all inputs and parameters of that system, through calculations proceeding *backwards* from outputs to

inputs. It permits local implication on parallel hardware(or wet-ware).

2. Backpropagation is any technique for adapting the weights or parameters of a nonlinear system by somehow using such derivatives or the equivalent.

Backpropagation has been considered one of the most important contributions to connectionist research. It actually allows the training of multi-layered networks and even applies to any differentiable or nonlinear system(for more on back-propagation, see [Werbos 1995]).

Brain-style computation may be also characterized by its features of (1)massively parallel computation, (2)constraint satisfaction, (3)cooperative computation, (4)distributed representation, and (5)content-addressable memory([Arbib 1987; Rumelhart 1989; Churchland & Sejnowski 1989; Smolensky 1988; Lippman 1987; Feldman & Ballard 1982]). But this characteristic itself does not directly show what neural computability means in contrast with Turing computability.

Gödel defined the computability of function on natural numbers as follows:

A function of integers is computable in any formal system containing arithmetic if and only if it is computable in arithmetic, where a function f is called computable in S if there is in S a computable term representing f. ([Gödel 1946])

A function is said to be Turing computable if its value can be computed by some Turing machine. Similarly, a function is neural computable if its value can be computed by a neural network. Accordingly, as McCulloch and Pitts remarked,

It is easily shown: first that every net[work], if furnished with a tape, scanners connected to afferents, and suitable efferents to perform the necessary motor-operartions, can compute only such numbers as can a Turing machine; second, that each of the latter numbers can be computed by such a net[work]; and that net[work]s with circles can compute, without scanners and a tape, some of the numbers the machine can, but no others, and not all of them([McCulloch & Pitts 1943]).

It is also well known that the MP neural network is equivalent to finite automata([Kleene 1956]) and that any finite state machine can be simulated by a MP neural network([Arbib 1964; Minsky 1967]). Thus, any computation by a Turing machine can be performed by a neural network([Franklin & Garzon 1991]).

The input-output relation in the McCulloch-Pitts neural network acts as a kind of Boolean function. Thus there are non-computable functions such as XOR function, i.e., the exclusive or predicate([Minsky & Papert 1988]). However, McCulloch-Pitts neural network can compute any Boolean function, (1) if the interaction of inputs to neurons is allowed for the given McCulloch-Pitts neural network([Arbib 1964]); and (2) if the hidden units are employed([Rumelhart, Hinton, & Williams 1986]). Hence, neural networks are at least as powerful as Turing machines.

A finite neural network FNN computes a Boolean function b if for all $x_1, ..., x_n \in \{0, 1\}$, the outputs of FNN on inputs are $b(x_1, ..., x_n)$. I. Parberry shows that every Boolean function can be computed by a uniform neural network family([Paberry 1996]). With an infinite family of finite neural networks, we obtain one with 1 input, one with 2 inputs, etc.

This uniform network family may have various resource bounds placed on it. Since the halting function for Turing machines is a Boolean function, it is computable in a uniform neural network family. According to Parberry, this unreasonable result comes from the fact that the interconnection pattern (V, E) and the gate assignment function can be non-computable functions. This style model is called a *nonuniform* circuit. In this case, however, we should assume the infinite class of finite neural networks.

Mathematically, neural networks with even Boolean weights are more powerful than the Turing machines. According to McCulloch and Pitts([1943]), McCulloch-Pitts neural network is equivalent to Turing machine. That is, all finite arithmetic calculation by Turing machine can be carried out in a neural network([Minsky 1967, Arbib 1987]).

Let S be the set of all Turing machines which compute

functions on the natural numbers. Clearly, S is countable. Define the function h such that

$$h : S \times \mathrm{N} \to \{0,1\}$$

called the halting function as follows:

$$h(x,y) = 1$$

if and only if xth Turing machine halts on the yth input. And the function $g : S \times \mathrm{N} \to \{0,1\}$ defined by $g(x) = h(x,x)$ for all $x \in \mathrm{N}$ such that

$$g(x) = 0$$

if and only if $h(x,y) = 1$.

Then halting function for Turing machine is computable in a neural network. We can construct a neural network to compute the halting function defined above. Consider neural computable function h, g and Turing computable function f, as follows:

$$h(x,y) = f(x,y,1)$$
$$g(x)f(x,0) \text{ if and only if } f(x,y,1).$$

Then $f(x,y,x,a) = (h(x,y) \wedge (a=1)) \wedge (g(x) \wedge (a=0))$.

Since h and g are computable by a neural network, f is computable by that neural network.

The computability of these neural networks has been explored by scholars such as S. Franklin and M. Garzon [1996], and H. Siegelmann and E. Sontag [1992]. Franklin and Garzon prove that the halting problem for the Turing machine is solvable in an infinite recurrent Boolean neural network. These scholars have shown remarkably that an infinite recurrent neural network solves the halting problem for the Turing machine. The halting function is thus computable in this neural network and hence, the computation power of neural networks is greater than Turing computability([Garzon 1995]).

However, this result is possible because of the infinite property in their neural network model. If we extend formal neurons to have real-valued states adjustable with infinite precision, then neural networks not only can simulate Turing machines but also even compute the non-computable([Arbib 1995], 34). Similarly, this property of infinitude gives rise to a certain Turing computability of the halting function if the uncountable infinity for the oracle Turing machine is allowed. It is possible to consider the use of the non-deterministic operations and oracle as a means of extending the Turing machine.

Siegelmann and Sontag prove that any function computable by a Turing machine can be computed by a finite recurrent neural network with rational weights([Siegelmann & Sontag 1992]). They show that their model can simulate a multitape Turing machine in linear time. According to Siegelmann and Sontag, the powerful activation functions of a finite neural network show superior computability to Turing machines if we allow infinite directed graphs. Although this argument is convincing, we should note that the result is based on the condition of infinite neural network, not the finitary condition.

I agree with Siegelmann and Sontag that if weights and activation functions are allowed to assume arbitrary real values, then neural networks with a certain continuous activation function are able to compute more effectively than the Turing machine. This is not, however, exactly within the scope of our discussion concerning neural computability and Gödel's results, for they assume the analog and stochastic computation of a recurrent neural network with rational weights and employ an unlimited memory([Siegelmann 1998]).

If all of the results of neural computability discussed here are accepted for the computability of the mind, one could clearly say that the mental computability of a neural network goes beyond the mental computability of a Turing machine. However, for a rigorous analysis of mental computability as neural computability, we must investigate the consistency of the finite neural networks that have been specified.

4.4 Consistency and Order of Neural Network

Gödel suggested:

A formal system can simply be defined to be any mechanical formulas, called provable formulas([Gödel 1964], 370).

On this point, for any formal system, there may exist a mechanical procedure which has the same provable formulas if the finite procedure is regarded as the mechanical procedure.

Neural networks may correspond to the biological model of computation, whereas Turing machines may correspond to the recursive logical model of computation. However, formal systems such as propositional calculus and first-order calculus can be implemented in neural networks.

According to McCulloch and Pitts [1943], there are the following physical assumptions for neurons:

1. The activity of the neuron is an all-or-none process.

2. A certain fixed number of synapses must be excited within the period of latent addition in order to excite a neuron at any time, and this number is independent of previous activity and position on the neuron.

3. The only significant delay within the nervous system is synaptic delay.

4. The activity of any inhibitory synapse absolutely prevents

excitation of the neuron at the time.

5. The structure of the neural network does not change with time.

Although these oversimplified assumptions were first introduced to feed-forward and unweighted networks, they provided a basic idea for alternatively understanding cognition from a formal perspective. Based on these assumptions they showed that any statement in propositional logic could be represented by a network of their formal neurons. McCulloch and Pitts [1943] concluded that the fundamental operations in psychology and physiology could be predicates of a two-valued logic.

For a rigorous discussion on implementation of logical systems in neural networks, we need to establish a kind of reduction or simplification as an assumption for our model.

ASSUMPTION. Fundamental hypothesis in setting up our model is that all the functioning of the nervous system relevant to our study is mediated solely by the passage of electrical impulses by cells we call neuron([Arbib 1987]).

This hypothesis implies that a collection of neurons can produce cognitive behavior such as mathematical thinking.

ACTIVATION RULE. A neuron fires only if the total

weight of the synapses that receive impulses in the period of latent summation exceeds the threshold of the neuron.

Here, the neurons can be viewed as computing units that evaluate a function of finite arguments.

We also need an inference rule since we consider a neural network as a formal model of the brain. This neuro-physiological activation rule is taken as the rule of inference in our model, whereas two rules such as *Modus Ponens* and *Generalization* are taken as the rules of inference in the first-order predicate calculus. By Modus Ponens and Generalization, we mean

(1) Modus Ponens: From A and $A \rightarrow B$ infer B.

(2) Generalization: If the variable x does not occur free in A, then

    (2-1) From $A \rightarrow B(x)$ infer $A \rightarrow \forall x B(x)$,

    (2-2) From $B(x) \rightarrow A$ infer $\exists x B(x) \rightarrow A$.

From this rule we can obtain primitive logical functions. For instance, the following recursive functions can be implemented in neural networks:

1. Negation $\neg$. Let $\neg$ be a unary negation function. Then $\neg : \{0,1\}^n \rightarrow \{0,1\}$ is a neural activation function such that $\neg(x_i) = \neg x_i$ for a natural number n.

2. Conjunction $\wedge$. Let $\wedge$ be an n-ary conjunction function. Then $\wedge : \{0,1\}^n \to \{0,1\}$ is a neural activation function such that

$$\wedge (x_1,...,x_n) = x_1 \wedge \cdots \wedge x_n.$$

3. Disjunction $\vee$. Let $\wedge$ be an n-ary disjunction function. Then $\vee : \{0,1\}^n \to \{0,1\}$ is a neural activation function such that

$$\vee (x_1,...,x_n) = x_1 \vee \cdots \vee x_n.$$

4. Implication $\to$. Let $\to$ be a binary implication function. Then $\to : \{0,1\}^n \to \{0,1\}$ is a neural activation function such that, (under the DeMorgan's laws)

$$\to (x_1,x_2) \quad \text{if and only if} \quad (\neg x_1 \vee x_2).$$

All the logical functions can be implemented with a network composed of units which compute the negation, conjuction, disjunction, implication functions. These examples show that the functions of first-order logic can be constructed by a neural network with some logical and non-logical axioms. If the network contains cycles, the computation may not be uniquely defined by the connection pattern. Thus, a certain input may produce a desired output, but how the network obtain this result is left to an emergent property.

Any logical function $f : \{0,1\}^n \rightarrow \{0,1\}$ can be computed with a McCulloch-Pitts network of two layers and hence, any logical function can be implemented in weighted neural networks.

4.5 Neural Network Beyond Gödel's Incompleteness

In this section, we assume some elementary results on models and cardinals. Proofs can be found in any text on mathematical logic([Barwise 1977; Barwise & Feferman 1985; Ebbinghaus 1985]).

As Gödel remarked,

··· due to A. M. Turing's work, a precise and unquestionably adequate definition of the general concept of formal system can now be given, the existence of undecidable arithmetical propositions and the non-demonstrability of the consistency of a system in the same system can now be proved rigorously for every consistent formal system containing a certain amount of finitary number theory(Italics in original, [Gödel 1964], 369).

This reflects that the application of Gödel's incompleteness theorems to a formal neural network requires that one first discuss the consistency of neural networks. In mathematics, the consistency condition is a minimal assumption of a theory. Thus arises the question: Is the formal system implemented in neural network a consistent system?

In order to analyze the consistency of the system of finite recurrent neural networks, we need to introduce some preliminary metamathematical theorems to classify the order of the systems. These theorems include the Compactness theorem, the Lőwenheim-Skolem theorem and the Lindström theorem.

THEOREM(The Compactness Theorem). Let S be a first-order system. Then, if every finite subset of S has a model then S has a model. The Compactness theorem states that a set of sentences has a model if and only if each finite subset of the set of sentences has a model.

THEOREM(The Lőwenheim-Skolem Theorem). Let S be a first-order system. Then there is a submodel of a model for S whose cardinality does not exceed that of S if S is infinite and is at most countable, if S is finite. The Lőwenheim-Skolem theorem shows that if a set of sentences has a model then it has an at most countable model.

THEOREM(The Lindström Theorem). 1. First-order logic is a maximal logic with respect to expressive power satisfying the Compactness theorem and the Lőwenheim-Skolem theorem.

2. First-order logic is a maximal logic satisfying the Completeness theorem and the Löwenheim-Skolem theorem.

In fact, this means that the first-order formal system is the only possible system when we do not employ the uncountability. The Lindström theorem proves that the first-order formal system is the maximal system that satisfies both the Compactness theorem and the Löwenheim-Skolem theorem.

We say that a class Γ of finite structures is first-order definable if Γ is defined by a first-order formal system. By the Lindström theorem, we can claim that the class of finite neural networks is not first-order definable. To do this, it is enough to prove that neural network is not a compact system if it is consistent. If a neural network is consistent, then it has a model, and hence all connection relations between nodes must be defined in neural networks. It is, however, observed that the collection of directed graphs of neural network is not first-order definable.

Let NN_{FR} be the class of finite recurrent neural networks. Then

1. The system of finite neurons in NN_{FR} is not first-order definable. Let S be a first-order system that defines the finite neurons n_i, and let

$$NN_{FR} = \{(n_0 = n_1) \vee (n_0 = n_2) \vee \cdots \vee (n_0 = n_i)\}$$

be an extension of S with a new axiom such that $n_0 \neq n_i$ $(0 < i < \aleph_0)$. Then

$$(n_0 = n_1) \vee (n_0 = n_2) \vee \cdots \vee (n_0 = n_i)$$

has no model, although every finite subset of NN_{FR} has a model. Hence, this is a counterexample to the compactness theorem.

2. There exists a connection that is not definable in NN_{FR}. Let $con_n(x,y)$ define the predicate expressing "there is a connection from node x to node y of length n." Then we have $\{\neg con_n(x,y) : n \geq 1\}$ which logically satisfies $\neg con_n(x,y)$, for constants a,b in NN_{FR}.

Suppose NN_{FR} is a first-order system. Then, by the Compactness theorem, there must be a natural number k such that

$$\{\neg con_n(a,b) : 1 \leq n \leq k\}$$

logically satisfies $\neg con_n(x,y)$. However, this is not valid. Hence, the predicate is not definable in the graphs of NN_{FR}. Consequently, the connection relation of NN_{FR} is not definable in NN_{FR}, and thus we have a contradiction. Hence, NN_{FR} is not a first-order system. In all, NN_{FR} is not compact.

Let NN_{FR} be a finite recurrent neural network. Then, in the representation power, NN_{FR} is more powerful than the first-order calculus system such as Peano Arithmetic and the

Turing machine([Hintikka 1994]). It is enough to show that NN_{FR} represents a Π_1^0 formula.

Branching Quantifier

Let $\triangle$ be any first-order structure which contains a copy of the natural numbers with addition and multiplication. For example, $\triangle$ might be some universe of set theory. Let $T_\triangle$ be the set of(Gödel numbers of $\lceil \varphi \rceil$) sentences φ in first-order language, which are true in $\triangle$. Then $T_\triangle$ is not Π_1^1 definable over $\triangle$, that is, not definable by a formula $\psi(x)$ of the form $\forall f_1 \cdots \forall f_n A(x, f_1, \ldots, f_n)$, where A is first-order and $f_1, \ldots, f_n$ are function symbols. This is even stronger than that $T_\triangle$ is not inductive. Since every inductive set is Π_1^1, but, in general, not conversely(if $\triangle$ is uncountable, e.g.)([Barwise 1979]).

To show that NN_{FR} represents a Π_1^0 formula, we introduce an expression with a branching quantifier, such as

$$\text{(a)} \quad \begin{array}{l} \forall x \searrow \\ \qquad\quad Computation\,[x,y] \\ \forall y \nearrow \end{array}$$

This expression (a) may be equivalent to some first-order formulas in linear forms:

$$\forall x \, \forall y \, Computation \, [x,y], \text{ or}$$

$$\forall y \, \forall x \, Computation \, [x,y].$$

However, we cannot know which first-order formula is exactly equivalent to the expression (b):

$$(b) \quad \forall x \diagdown \atop \exists y \diagup \quad Computation \, [x,y]$$

because two formulas,

$$\forall x \, \exists y \, Computation \, [x,y], \text{ and}$$

$$\exists y \, \forall x \, Computation \, [x,y].$$

are not logically equivalent, and the expression (b) must be treated at once.

Consequently, the meaning of a branching quantifier expression (c):

$$(c) \quad \forall x \, \exists y \diagdown \atop \exists u \, \exists w \diagup \quad Computation \, [x,y]$$

cannot be defined inductively in terms of first-order formulas by representing one quantifier at a time.

NN_{FR} represents a Π_1^0 formula. Take the formula $\forall y \neg Pf(x,y)$. The expression (d) is not representable in any first-order sequential computing system such that

$$\text{(d)} \quad \begin{matrix} \forall\, y_1 \neg Pf(x_1, y_1) \diagdown \\ \qquad\qquad Computation\,[x_1, y_1, x_2, y_2] \\ \forall\, y_2 \neg Pf(x_2, y_2) \diagup \end{matrix}$$

The expression (d) is equivalent to

$$\exists\, \varphi_1 \, \exists\, \varphi_2 \, Computation\,[x_1, \varphi_1(x_1), x, \varphi_2(x_2)].$$

This formula is not representable in the first-order systems since it is being quantified over a set of variables, that is, predicates or functions. However, (d) is representable in NN_{FR} because connectionist formal systems can compute many things simultaneously. Hence, NN_{FR} is not a first-order but second-order formal system. Moreover, even in the case of the Gödel sentence

$$Cons\,(NN_{FR}) \leftrightarrow \forall\, y \neg Pf(\gamma, y),$$

where γ is the Gödel number of $cons\,(NN_{FR})$, there is no reason why NN_{FR} cannot compute the Gödel sentence of NN_{FR}. Although $x_1 = x_2$, no contradiction appears.

NN_{FR} is not a first-order system. But suppose that NN_{FR} is a first-order system. By Gödel's Second Incompleteness Theorem, NN_{FR} is not a consistent system because it can compute such a Gödel sentence, which brings us to the following conclusion: either NN_{FR} is a first-order and inconsistent formal system or else a second-order formal system.

The disjunction seems inescapable: either the finite neural network NN_{FR} is not first-order consistent or else it is second-order. If the first alternative holds, then NN_{FR} can prove and compute everything, including logical paradoxes. However, if the second one is true, then the finite neural network NN_{FR} is beyond the limitations of the first-order calculus systems in that it represents and decides the undecidable sentence in the Π_1^0 class. This alternative implies that Gödel's speed-up theorem holds up in the neural network model, and that Gödel's doctrine can be demonstrated in the neural network model.

There are two distinct perspectives between Turing computability and neural computability, since a neural network cannot be axiomatized by a Turing machine. From the perspective of Turing computability, both human and artificial cognition are understood as a formal mapping definable by a Turing machine. If the human mind is a Turing machine, then Gödel's Incompleteness Theorems limit cognition in both.

A recurrent neural network can reflect Gödel's doctrine. From the perspective of neural computability, however, human and artificial cognition are considered as a formal mapping definable by a finite neural network. If human cognition is a finite recurrent neural network, then Gödel's incompleteness theorems do not limit cognition.

Rather, they show that cognition has not a first-order but a second-order property. Hence, in terms of the first-order, a neural network system is not consistent because it computes the undecidable sentence or the Halting function. In terms of the second-order, however, we can prove neither its consistency nor its inconsistency in a neural network system.

The parallel computing model shows that the cognition concept should reflect Gödel's doctrine, that is, what Gödel's incompleteness theorems would say. This is the capability to form an ever higher type, or higher order, over itself, which is referred to as metacomputability.

Within the context of the disjunction, Gödel's theorem itself neither separates human cognition from artificial cognition nor does it equalize the two cognitive systems. Rather, the theorem implies neither the Artificial Intelligence Thesis nor its negation. Gödel's incompleteness theorems are not inconsistent with Gödel's disjunction and with his doctrine.

If we want to specify the consistency of a cognitive system, we cannot prove or decide it by using this specified system. In this sense, the theorem is absolutely undecidable. However, if a higher type or axiom could be added to the previous system, its consistency would be decidable.

The concept of the computable finally depends upon the defined or specified system. For, if the cognitive system is definable by a Turing machine, it has Turing computability; whereas if the cognitive system is definable by a finite neural network, it has neural computability. Thus, if we accept the computability of minds as neural computability, Gödel's incompleteness theorems would be able to show the meta-computability of minds.

CHAPTER 5

Gödel's Cognitive Science

5.1 Gödel's Incompleteness and Mathematical Thinking

According to Roger Penrose, there are at least four viewpoints concerning the relationship between mathematical thinking and computation([Penrose 1994; 1997]):

A. All thinking is computation, in particular, feelings of conscious awareness are evoked merely by the carrying out of appropriate computations. Proponents of viewpoint A include Alan Turing, Allen Newell, Herbert A. Simon, John McCarthy, Marvin Minsky, Douglas Hofstadter.

B. Awareness is a feature of the brain's physical action; and, whereas any physical action can be simulated computationally, computational simulation cannot by itself evoke awareness. Viewpoint B has been promoted by John Searle.

C. Appropriate physical action of the brain evokes awareness, but this physical action cannot even be properly simulated computationally.

D. Awareness cannot be explained by physical, computational, or any other scientific terms.

Penrose then analyzes that Turing's viewpoint is contained within A, that is, the so-called Strong AI or computational functionalism, and Gödel's view in D, that is, the mystical category.

Penrose himself is a proponent of viewpoint C, especially Strong C rather than Weak C. According to Weak C, there is nothing we need to look for outside of what is currently known in physics in order to find the appropriate non-computational action. According to Strong C, however, there should be something outside known physics, which means our current knowledge of physics is insufficient for a complete understanding of greater awareness([Penrose 1997]).

In spite of Penrose's contribution to showing the relevance of Gödel and cognitive science, I do not agree with him on the interpretation of Gödel's mystical position. First, his classification is not satisfactory in that viewpoint A is directed toward computation and thinking; B toward physical action, computation, and thinking; C toward physical action, computation, and thinking; and D toward physical action, computation, and thinking. Thus, Penrose should have indicated at least eight viewpoints(that means 2^3) for a complete categorization. However, he does not give any reason as to why the remaining viewpoints are omitted.

Second, less convincing is Penrose's assertion that Gödel's viewpoint is mystical. Although he uses Gödel's own statements([Gödel 1951]) as evidence, the reference is very limited in that it does not show that Gödel refuted viewpoint A. Contrary to Penrose's claim, Gödel's conclusive disjunction([Gödel 1951]) can be viewed as being logically consistent not only with viewpoint D, but also with viewpoint A.

To understand Gödel's viewpoint and the implications of his celebrated incompleteness theorems for cognitive science, we need to address the his disjunction. According to Gödel, it is clearly inevitable with regard to both the human and artificial minds([Gödel 1951]).

Our concern shall be focused on the question of the computational property of cognition and its relation to Gödel's Incompleteness Theorems. From a formal perspective, the following question can be raised: *What can be computed by cognitive systems*; in particular, *what can be computed by neural networks*? Our approach will consist of stating and answering that question. By cognitive computability, we mean the computability of cognitive systems including minds, brains, and machines. Thus, an analysis of the notion of cognitive computability is essential to be able to answer the question.

Gödel defined the computability of function on natural numbers as follows:

A function of integers is computable in any formal system containing arithmetic if and only if it is computable in arithmetic, where a function f is called computable in S if there is in S a computable term representing f. ([Gödel 1946])

A function is computable in intuitive sense if and only if there is an effective procedure for computing the function. Here, the term *computation* includes, at least, three elements: storage, transmission, and processing. Computation can be viewed as a purely formal concept. The term *computability*, however, can be viewed as an intuitive concept rather than a purely formal concept.

The first formal justification of computability was proposed by Turing([1936]). He was analyzing what a human computer could do. Turing's definition of computability is now called *classical computability*. Another computational model was neural networks [McCulloch & Pitts 1943], as a formal model of computing brains, which, unlike Turing machines, do not operate sequentially. This model has the structure of neural systems and also means an alternative computability paradigm.

We, therefore, are required to examine the computability of neural networks for understanding the relationship between cognitive computability and Gödel's incompleteness.

5.2 Gödel's Incompleteness and Human Mind

The logical result of Gödel's theorems is clear. Cognitive scientists like D. Hofstadter([1979]) and R. Penrose([1987, 1994]) stress that Gödel's theorems may provide a fundamental key to understanding cognition and the nature of the mind. However, far from obvious remain the implications for the relationship between human cognition and artificial cognition.

A central concern of implications of Gödel's incompleteness theorems is centered around the question: *Is the human mind formally equivalent to the artificial mind?* A great amount, therefore, has been written on the mind-machine or brain-machine controversy: *Is the human mind, or the human brain, essentially superior to machines?* Despite the relevance of the content of their work, however, their assumptions and arguments do not converge. Only a few of the many works are representative.

Gödel's Theorems Limit Computing Machines Only

According to E. Nagel and J. R. Newman([1958]), J. R. Lucas([1961; 1996]), and R. Penrose([1989; 1990; 1994]), Gödel's Incompleteness Theorems would show that human cognition is beyond artificial cognition. All they assert is that the two cognitive systems cannot be equivalent.

This argument heavily relies on the theoretical assumption that human cognition can know the truth of Gödel sentences or can prove those theorems that cannot be proved by means of artificial cognition. However, because they employ other assumptions outside of Gödel's work, for example, the consistency of the actual mind, they fail to justify such an assumption.

J. R. Lucas: From his paper, *Minds, Machines, and Gödel* ([1961]), Lucas begins and continues the Mind-Machine problem with Gödel's Incompleteness Theorems. He asserts: Gödel's theorem seems to me to prove that Mechanism is false, that is, that minds cannot be explained as machines.

LUCAS' ARGUMENT: No computing machine can be equivalent to a human mathematician.

We can analyze this argument as follows: Let M^* be the

set of theorems listed by the mechanized formal system M, and H^* the set of sentences that the human mathematical intuition H will ever be in a position to assert as truth. If $M^* \subseteq H^*$, then H can see that M embodies a true formal system. If H knows that M is true, then H knows that M is inconsistent, and the consistency of M denoted by $cons(M)$, is in H^*. By Gödel's second incompleteness theorem, we obtain $cons(M)$ is not in M^*. Thus, $M^* \neq H^*$ if $M^* \subseteq H^*$. Of course, $M^* \neq H^*$ if $M^* \supset H^*$. Hence, no M is equivalent to H ([Rucker 1995]).

However, his conclusion directly come from his strong assumption, not from a proof. Thus, we can obtain the negation of the result by replacing M^* with H^*. What he asserts is that a mechanical model must be finite and definite and then mind can always go one better, because a human mathematician can know the truth of Gödel sentences but the machine cannot. But Lucas seems to fail to explain the definition of the term *know*. His argument depends on an unfair assumption. For the major critiques of Lucas' argument, see Rucker ([1995]), Yu([1992]), Webb([1980; 1990]), Nelson([1987]), and Hofstadter([1979]).

P. Benacerraf: In his article, *God, the devil, and Gödel* [1967], Benacerraf reconstructed Lucas argument. He contends that Lucas argument failed to establish as anti-mechanistic conclusion. Benacerraf suggested that Gödel's incompleteness theorems imply that if human mathematicians are Turing machines, they cannot know which machines they are.

However, the issue of the consistency of the human mind still remains unsolved, because such an assumption depends on the individual. Some of the scholars who argue against Lucas stand in line with Benacerraf: Putnam([1964]), Good([1969]), Chihara([1972]).

R. Penrose: Penrose provoked a hot debate([see *Behavioral and Brain Sciences* 13, 1990; *Psyche* 2, 1995]) when he posited computation as a finitely described procedure, that is, a decision procedure. Penrose maintains that human mind cannot be a computing machine.

PENROSE'S ARGUMENT([1994]). Human mathematicians are not using a knowably sound algorithm in order to ascertain mathematical truth.

By showing the computational limitation of the Turing machine model, he argues that human mathematicians are not using a knowably sound algorithm in order to ascertain mathematical truth. His argument has its own roots in the following theorem.

THEOREM([Penrose 1994]). Suppose TM is a Turing machine which is such that whenever TM halts on an input (q,n) then the qth computation $Computation_q(n)$ does not halt. Then for some k, $Computation_k(k)$ does not halt, but TM does not halt on (k,k).

There is no essential difference between Penrose's theorem and Turing's theorem [1936]. S. Feferman [1995] pointed out that this theorem is equivalent to Kleene's Theorem XIII([Kleene 1952], 302):

If a formal system is sound for the predicate, then it is not complete for it.

These theorems claim that the soundness of a formal system implies its incompleteness.

According to Penrose, the mind is something that cannot be described in any kind of computational terms. He uses Gödel's incompleteness theorems to show that mathematical understanding is something beyond computation.

I agree with Penrose that the implications of Gödel's theorem for cognitive science has a significant effect, but I disagree with him that he disregards (1) Gödel's own view on that problem and (2) the differences between neural networks and Turing machines in the computational nature. His controversial term knowably sound algorithm does not, in fact, include a parallel and adaptive computation.

In contrast to Penrose's analysis of the mind as a computational concept, his work treats the brain as merely a physical concept although he recognizes the significance of the brain in the science of consciousness. For the major critiques of Penrose's argument, see LaForte, Hayes, & Ford([1998]); Copeland([1998]); Feferman([1995]); Williamson([1996]); McCarthy([1995]); Putnam([1995]); Minsky([1991b]).

Gödel's Theorems Do Not Limit Computing Machines Only

Mathematical logician E. Post had already claimed that there is a fundamental discovery in the limitations of the formalizing powers of Homo Sapiens([Post 1936]). Post held the view that Gödel's incompleteness theorems imply the existence of problems absolutely unsolvable for the human mind. But he did not provide a proof.

Cognitive scientists such as D. Hofstadter([1979]), M. A. Arbib([1987]), and H. A. Simon([1989]) have asserted that Gödel's theorems not only limit artificial cognition but also human cognition, or they limit human cognition as much as artificial cognition. Thus Gödel's theorems do not imply that human cognition is superior to artificial cognition.

H. A. Simon and C. A. Kaplan: Simon and Kaplan [1989] take a neutral position. They state that,

The Gödel theorems have often been the basis for arguments on the limits of computers. These results show that in rich systems of logic, certain theorems, known to be true by reasoning in a metalanguage, cannot be proved within the logic itself. What is sometimes overlooked is that the Gödel theorems are wholly neutral as between people and computers, placing just as strict but no more strict limits on one as on the other. Hence the implications of the incompleteness theorems for the question of machine intelligence are still quite uncertain([Simon & Kaplan 1989], 36).

M. A. Arbib: In his book, *Brains, Machines, and Mathematics* [1964; 1987], Arbib argues against those philosophers who assert that Gödel's incompleteness theorems inherently limit the possible intelligence of machines. He treats this subject in a rather different light:

First, Arbib uses the term *brain*, not mind.

Second, he points out that Gödel's incompleteness theorems only place limitations upon consistent minds or machines. According to Arbib, if both the mind and the machine are consistent, then Gödel's theorems do limit a human as much as a machine. However, he strongly doubts that human beings are consistent. In this case, Gödel's theorem is not relevant to the brain-machine controversy. He concludes that Gödel's theorem does not imply a negative answer to the questions: *Is a person a machine?* or *Could a machine be cognitive?*

Third, Arbib contends that Gödel's theorem can be removed incrementally in a mechanical way in what is referred to as a *speed-up*, which is the adding of an undecidable Gödel sentence to an incomplete logic system. He introduced the proof-measure system to prove that if a system can do some things arbitrarily quicker than , then can do some things that cannot do at all. Thus, Arbib claimed that,

If we add an undecidable axiom to an incomplete logic, not only are there truths that become theorems for the first time, but also theorems that were already provable in the old system may have shorter proofs in the new system([Arbib 1987], 187).

His argument is convincing, and he goes far beyond others in the use of Gödel's theorem. Arbib's contribution is the combination of adding new axioms to a logic system with adding new instructions to a computing machine. This application is appropriate within the context of our discussion on Gödel's theorem.

A. E. Lygzeidetson: In his paper, *Abstract Complexity Theory and the Mind-Machine Problem*([1994]), Lyngzeidetson asserts that Gödel's speed-up phenomenon show that the human mind is not limited by Gödel's incompleteness theorems. He interprets the mind as an *open* system interacting with an environment that contains non-computability. He also maintain that machines as open systems can not be limited by Gödel's theorem.

However, his argument and use of the speed-up theorem is not convincing in that he does not clarify what machines could be open systems and what machines could contain non-computability.

Rather, in his 1990 paper, *Massively Parallel Distributed Processing and a Computationalist Foundation for Cognitive Science*, it is worth noting that Lyngzeidetson introduces the term *connection machine* or parallel distributed processing model. He, however, did not distinguish between connection machines and connectionist machines. For the connection machine may be viewed as a collection of serial machines, whereas the connectionist machine is a parallel machine that operates simultaneously. He conjectures that connection machines can go beyond Penrose's argument. This possibility, however, is only based on the negation of the limitation of serial architecture.

R. Rucker: In his book, *Infinity and the Mind* [1995], Rucker introduces the famous Berry's Paradox to disprove the Lucas and Penrose-style argument. He attempt to show that $H^{*} = M_{h}^{*}$

is compatible with Gödel's incompleteness theorems, if the large natural and humanly nameable number is greater than the human Berry number, which is the first number that the human mind cannot find a name for (where M^* is the set of theorems listed by the mechanized formal system M, and H^* the set of sentences that the human mathematical intuition H will ever be in a position to assert as truths).

According to Rucker, it is not unreasonable to expect that a machine be identical to human mathematical cognition. Although his argument is convincing, the idea is based on the speed concept, that is, the ratio of evolution, not on computational power.

N. Shankar: Although he does not directly deal with our issue in his *Metamathematics, Machines, and Gödel's Proof* [1994], Shankar in LISP programming terms proves that the Boyer-Moore theorem prover is able to verify a proof of Gödel's first incompleteness theorem. This implies that the theorem can be no longer a consequence that the algorithm cannot reach.

A great amount has been written on the implications of Gödel's incompleteness theorems for the mind and machine equivalence problem. However, most studies on cognitive computability and Gödel's incompleteness have been done with the Turing machine model from a symbolic perspective. For them, a computing machine just means Turing machines, not artificial neural networks. Thus, neither in their arguments nor in their methodologies do any of the aforementioned scholars go beyond the concerns centered around the problem of neural computability and Gödel's own view.

5.3 Gödel's Speed-up Theorem

Gödel maintained that higher types allow one to prove undecidable Gödel sentences in systems of lower levels([Gödel 1936]). A general study of the speed-up phenomenon in terms of proofs appears in Statman([Statman 1978]). The term speed-up is not due to Gödel himself but was introduced by Blum([Blum 1967]) in terms of complexity theory in computer science. This phenomenon became a major topic in theoretical computer science and, indeed, the celebrated $P = NP?$ problem can itself be thought of as a speed-up problem([Parikh 1986]).

Let S_i be the system of logic of the ith order, the natural numbers being taken as individuals. Then S_i contains the appropriate logical axioms, variables and quantifiers for natural numbers, for classes of natural numbers, for classes of classes of natural numbers, and so on, up to classes of the ith type, but no variables of a higher type. Then, there are properties of S_i that are provable in S_{i+1} but not in S_i.

On the other hand, if we consider those formulas that are provable in S_i as well as S_{i+1}, then the following holds: For each function φ that is computable in S_i there exist infinitely many formulas A such that if k is the length of a shortest proof of A in S_i and l is the length of a shortest proof of A in S_{i+1}, then $k > \varphi(l)$. He concluded that

Thus, passing to the logic of the next higher order has the effect, not only of making provable certain propositions that were not provable before, but also of making it possible to shorten, by an extraordinary amount, infinitely many of the proofs already available.(Italics in original, [Gödel 1936], 397).

The main result is that there are formulas that can be proved both in S_i and S_{n+1} but whose shortest proof in S_{n+1} is much shorter than that in S_i. Thus, by successively adding a higher type one arrives at a sequence of ever stronger systems. In fact, Gödel already addressed the speed-up issue in his previous papers([Gödel 1931; 1932b]). He maintained that higher types allow one to prove Gödel sentences undecidable in systems of lower levels.

According to M. Arbib, Gödel's incompleteness can be removed incrementally in a mechanical way in what is referred to as a speed-up, which is analogous to adding of an undecidable sentence, such as a Gödel sentence, to an incomplete logic system([Arbib 1987]).

Arbib introduced the proof-measure system to prove that if a system S_1 can do some things arbitrarily quicker than S, then S_1 can do some things that S cannot do at all. Gödel's speed-up theorem is relevant for increasing the range of the computing machine by adding new instructions. Arbib remarks:

If we add an undecidable axiom to an incomplete logic, not only are there truths that become theorems for the first time, but also theorems that were already provable in the old system may have shorter proofs in the new system([1987], 187).

Arbib's contribution here is the combination of adding new axioms to a logic system with adding new instructions to a computing machine. It seems to me a proper application of Gödel's theorems to cognitive science. Nevertheless, the finite description issue and the consistency issue of cognitive systems in effect remain unresolved. For, there is a critical difference between [Gödel 1931] and [Gödel 1936].

In his paper [1936], Gödel allowed *infinitely* many proofs with a given number of lines, whereas he allowed only *finitely* many proofs with a given number of symbols in his work [Gödel 1931]. Furthermore, in order to rigorously analyze the implications of Gödel's theorems for cognitive systems, we need to address not only the Turing machine model, but also the neural network model.

This presents two problems to the cognitive scientist. One is the disregard for the computational model of neural networks. The other is the erroneous application of Gödel's incompleteness theorems to the issue of cognition in natural or artificial systems.

One of the best ways to avoid these problems is to analyze Gödel's own view on both the human and artificial minds. To understand Gödel's viewpoint is one thing, to use Gödel's theorems is another. It is thus necessary to precisely distinguish Gödel's own argument from, the so-called Gödelian arguments([Lucas 1961]), in which many scholars just use Gödel's results without addressing Gödel's original intention.

5.4 Gödel's Doctrine

The speed-up theorem implies that a certain function has no best algorithms. S. Feferman [1998] articulates the speed-up aspects of Gödel's incompleteness theorems from Gödel's own footnote 48a([Gödel 1931]), in which Gödel clarified:

As will be shown in Part II of this paper, the true reason for the incompleteness inherent in all formal systems of mathematics is that the formation of ever higher types can be continued into the transfinite (see Hilbert 1926, ["Über das Unendliche", Mathematische Annalen 95, 161-190], 184), while in any formal system at most denumerably many of them are available. For it can be shown that the undecidable propositions constructed here become decidable whenever appropriate higher types are added(for example, the type ω to the system P). An analogous situation prevails for the axiom of set theory([Gödel 1931], 181).

Feferman then calls it *Gödel's doctrine:* wherein the unlimited transfinite iteration of the power-set operation is necessary to account for finitary mathematics. He asserts that the *true reason* for the incompleteness phenomena is that the formation of ever higher types can be continued into the transfinite, both in systems explicitly using types and in systems of set theory, such as ZF(Zermelo-Fraenkel set theory), for which the(cumulative) type structure is implicit in the axioms([Feferman 1998], 229]).

Axioms of ZF:

(ZF1) *Axiom of Extensionality.* If X and Y have the same elements, then $X = Y$.

(ZF2) *Axiom of Pairing.* For any a and b there exists a set $\{a,b\}$ that contains exactly a and b.

(ZF3) *Axiom Schema of Separation.* If φ is a property (with parameter p), then for any X and p there exists a set $Y = \{u \in X : \varphi(u,p)\}$ that contains all those $u \in X$ that have the property φ.

(ZF4) *Axiom of Union.* For any X there exists a set $Y = \cup X$, the union of all elements of X.

(ZF5) *Axiom of Power Set.* For any X there exists a set $Y = \wp(X)$, the set of all subsets of X.

(ZF6) *Axiom of Infinity.* There exists an infinite set.

(ZF7) *Axiom of Schema of Replacement.* If f is a function, then for any X there exists a set $Y = f[X] = \{f(x) : x \in X\}$.

(ZF8) *Axiom of Regularity.* Every nonempty set has an $\in$-minimal element.

Thus one can obtain a new Π_1^0 sentence by adding a higher type to the fixed system. Along this line of thought, Feferman([1962]) studied the transfinite recursive and concluded that even a higher type formation cannot be established by the incompleteness property alone([Feferman 1994]). Following Gödel([1946], 150),

      $\cdots$ there exist certain negative results, such as the incompleteness of every formalism or the paradox of Richard. But closer examination shows that *these results do not make a definition of the absolute notions concerned impossible under all circumstances,* but only exclude certain ways of defining them, or, at least, that certain very closely related concepts may be definable in an absolute sense(Italics in mine).

Thus, Gödel's incompleteness theorems do not absolutely close the door to prove consistency if Hilbert's restrictions with respect to finite procedures are abandoned. Rather, they open the possibility of further attempts to prove the consistency of formal systems by adding new axioms and theorems. From this perspective, consistency proof is not a matter of ultimate mathematical truth, but of relative truth.

In his *The Consistency of the Axiom of Choice and of the Generalized Continuum Hypothesis* [Gödel 1940], finally, Gödel proved that if the set theory - whose axioms are those of the von Neumann-Bernays system except the axiom of choice - is consistent, then the theory obtained by adding a strong form of the axiom of choice and the generalized continuum hypothesis to these axioms is also consistent.

Axiom of Choice: Every family of nonempty sets has a choice function.

Generalized Continuum Hypothesis: For any α, $2^{\aleph_\alpha} = \aleph_{\alpha+1}$.

In his *On Completeness and Consistency* [Gödel 1932], Gödel generalized his incompleteness theorem and its mathematical meaning as follows:

> To be sure, all the propositions thus constructed are expressible in Z(hence are number-theoretic propositions); they are, however, not decidable in Z, but only in higher systems, for example, in that of analysis. In case we adopt a type-free construction of mathematics, as is done in the axiom system of set theory, axioms of cardinality(that is, axioms postulating the existence of sets of ever higher cardinality) take the place of the type extensions, and it follows that certain arithmetic propositions that are undecidable in Z become decidable by axioms of cardinality, for example, by the axiom that there exist sets whose cardinality is greater than every α_n, where $\alpha_0 = \aleph_0$, $\alpha_{n+1} = 2^{\alpha_n}$([Gödel 1932], 237).

In essence, we cannot approach the real meaning of Gödel's incompleteness theorems without addressing the concept of higher systems.

5.5 Gödel's Disjunctive Conclusion

There exist two alternatives on the equivalence of the mind and the machine. In 1951, Gödel delivered the 25th Josiah Willard Gibbs Lecture, entitled *Some Basic Theorems on the*

Foundations of Mathematics and Their Implications [Gödel 1951], at the American Mathematical Society.

In this talk, Gödel addressed the significance of the incompleteness theorems for the controversies surrounding the nature of mathematics and the limitations of human cognition. He focused on the fundamental issue of the human mind and mechanical objects. Gödel asserted that the following disjunctive conclusion is inevitable with respect to the undecidable:

Either mathematics is incompletable in this sense, that its evident axioms can never be comprised in a finite rule, that is to say, the human mind(even within the realm of pure mathematics) infinitely surpasses the powers of any finite machine, or else there exist absolutely unsolvable diophantine problems of the type specified(where the case that both terms of the disjunction are true is not excluded, so that there are, strictly speaking, three alternatives). It is this mathematically established fact which seems to me of great philosophical interest(Italics in original, [Gödel 1951], 310).

For Gödel, it is *intuitionists* in the foundation of mathematics who assert the first alternative of the disjunction and negate the second part. Gödel regarded *finitists* as opponents of the first disjunctive term. Epistemologically, these terms are more precise expressions rather than mechanism or anti-mechanism. Thus for the intuitionist or finitist, the theorem holds as an implication instead of a disjunction([Gödel 1951], footnote 15).

Such a disjunctive conclusion illustrates that Gödel's position cannot be reduced to a mystical one. Rather, according to Gödel's interpretation, Penrose would be classified as an intuitionistic mathematician, and Turing a finitistic mathematician.

Moreover, the disjunction may clarify some of the controversial terms in cognitive science, such as mechanism and anti-mechanism, or AI thesis and anti-AI thesis. Mechanism is the thesis asserting that the human mind and the brain are machines. The AI thesis states: As the intelligence of machines evolves, its underlying mechanisms will gradually converge to the mechanisms underlying human intelligence([Hofstadter, 1979]).

Scholars like Hao Wang [1974; 1996], Rudy Rucker [1995], and Stewart Shapiro [1998] have concerned themselves with Gödel's disjunction and Gödel's view on human and artificial cognition. Wang [1996] convincingly argued that Gödel affirmed neither *computabilism* nor *neuralism* as being true. Here, computabilism is the thesis that the brain and the mind function basically like a computing machine. Neuralism is the thesis that the brain suffices to explain mental phenomena([Wang 1996]).

We should note, however, that Gödel presupposed the brain to be a machine. Therefore, the term neuralism refers simply to Turing computabilism or a physical theory, rather than contemporary brain theories.

The First Alternative

The first alternative is that the mind is superior to the machine, whereas the second shows that there is no mind beyond the machine. Suppose that Gödel's second incompleteness theorem is true in both the human mind and any finite machine. Then there is a proposition decidable by the human mind, yet undecidable by any finite machine.

A clear example of this is the proposition expressing the consistency of finite machines. In this sense, mathematics is *incompletable* because mathematics cannot be embodied in a finite rule. For Gödel, this consequently implies that the human mind cannot be reducible to any finite describable machine. Accordingly, there is no essential difference between the first alternative and Penrose's argument.

Namely, if the first alternative holds, this seems to imply that the working of the human mind cannot be reduced to the working of the brain, which to all appearances is a finite machine with a finite number of parts, namely, the neurons and their connections([Gödel 1951], 311).

This first alternative, however, does not necessarily mean that the incompleteness theorems preclude the existence of an idealized AI produced by a finite rule. Rather, the theorems say that if there is such a finite rule then we will be unable to recognize it as such.

It is not known whether the first alternative holds, but at any rate it is in good agreement with the opinions of some of the leading men in brain and nerve physiology, who very decidedly deny the possibility of a purely mechanistic explanation of psychical and nervous process([Gödel 1951], 312).

Gödel never asserted that the first alternative holds only in terms of his incompleteness theorems.

The Second Alternative

For the second alternative proposition, Gödel's theorem shows that there exists an undecidable proposition for both the human mind and any finite machine if *a specified type* is allowed; otherwise we cannot use Gödel's results. This is an essential point in the application of Gödel's theorems to the issues being discussed here. Therefore, there is no essential difference between this alternative and Turing's argument that mental procedures cannot go beyond mechanical procedures.

Gödel asserted that the first alternative seems to imply that

··· mathematical objects and facts(or at least something in them) exist objectively and independently of our mental acts and decision(Italics in original, [Gödel 1951], 311).

For Gödel, this case disproves the view that mathematics is merely our own creation. However, to verify this alternative, we must first specify the type of system.

In his work([Gödel 1972]), Gödel pointed out that Turing's argument - mental procedures cannot go beyond mechanical procedures - is inconclusive. Gödel claimed that

Turing completely disregarded the fact that mind, in its use, is not static, but constantly developing, i.e., that we understand abstract terms more and more precisely as we go on using them([Gödel 1972], 306).

Gödel, therefore, did not accept Turing's argument. From the viewpoint of the incompleteness theorems, however, Gödel never claimed that they refuted Turing's mechanistic view of the mind, which is a different assertion altogether. He asserted only that the disjunctive conclusion must hold.

Since both terms of the disjunction are true is not excluded, the third alternative follows. Gödel focused on the disjunction, whereas intuitionists and finitists focused on only one alternative term of the disjunction. They would regard Gödel's conclusion not as a disjunction but as an implication.

Gödel, however, never claimed that the incompleteness theorems refute one alternative view of the mind. Rather, he refuted such an logical implication. According to Gödel([1951]), the disjunctive conclusion must hold:

Either (1) the human mind infinitely surpasses the powers of any finite machine, or else (2) there exist absolutely unsolvable diophantine problems.

Gödel's own interpretations allowed a corresponding disjunction:

Either (1') the working of the human mind cannot be reduced to the working of a finite machine, or else (2') mathematical objects and facts exist objectively and independently of our acts and decision.

Those alternatives were not mutually exclusive. On this point, I agree with Dawson([1997]) that, indeed, Gödel was firmly convinced of the truth of both. Thus, follows a disjunction for cognitive science that

Either (1") the working of human mind cannot be reduced to the working of a Turing machine, or else (2") Gödel sentences exist independently of our cognition.

Gödel's disjunctive conclusion actually disclosed a new problem rather than supporting one specific alternative. Thus, we cannot say that Gödel's incompleteness theorems imply that the human mind is superior to the artificial mind. His conclusion ever stands in contrast with a fixed alternative. Gödel just opened the wider door to the science of the mind.

Quantum Cognitive Science

All the classical computing system can not be free from Gödel's incompleteness theorems. His incompleteness theorems imply the necessity of the non-deterministic quantum computation beyond the deterministic computation([Blaha 2005]).

If we offer a new projection from all the classical models to the mind at the quantum level, then we construct a quantum cognitive science. How to capture the quantum computing model inherent in cognitive science is very interesting and challenging([Goertzel 1993]). Given the current models in cognitive science, we are interested in how to gain some insights about the definition of quantum cognitive science from quantum computing.

Quantum computing is theoretically based on quantum system with finite dimensional Hilbert spaces, especially the state space of a qubit, $\mathbb{C}^2$. The quantum logic by G. Birkhoff and J. von Neumann is based on the lattice of closed subspaces of a Hilbert space([Birkhoff & von Neumann 1936]). Since the distribution law does not hold in the quantum logic of $\mathbb{C}^2$, therefore, the quantum logic of $\mathbb{C}^2$ is different from that of $\mathbb{C}$, hence different from Turing machines equivalent to the first order logic([Dunn, Hagge, Moss, Wang 2005]).

Now, classical cognitive science can be defined in terms of projections as follows:

Symbolic Projection $\cap$ Connectionist Projection.

Then quantum cognitive science can be defined as follows:

Quantum Symbolic Projection $\cap$ Quantum Connectionist Projection.

Can cognition be the results of quantum computing on the part of neurons? A new step for cognitive science has been developing ever since the discovery of quantum theory. A hypothesized quantum approach is also intended as architectures of mind([Stapp 2004; Hiley 1997; Penrose 1994; Goertzel 1994; Hodgson 1991; Lockwood 1989]).

Proposition.

1. *mind* $\leftrightarrow$ $f(quantum\ physical\ reality)$

2. *quantum physical reality* $\leftrightarrow$ $g(mind)$,

for some mappings f and g.

This means:

1. Mind is defined in some way by quantum physical reality

2. Quantum physical reality is defined in some way by mind.

Quantum theoretical concepts are relevant to the understanding of the human mind([Kak 1992]). For example, the metacomputational aspects of cognition may be related to the metacomputational processes which are involved in the quantum reduction of the wavefunction to macroscopic observables. Beyond Gödel's disjunctive conclusion, we are now faced with the problem of how to regard questions as a metacomputability of the mind in the light of the quantum results.

Bibliography

[Amari 1990] S. Amari, *Mathematical Foundations of Neurocomputing*, **Proceedings of IEEE**, 78(9): 1443-1463.

[Anderson & Rosenfeld 1988] J. A. Anderson and E. Rosenfeld (eds.), **Neurocomputing: Foundation of Research**, Cambridge: The MIT Press.

[Arbib & Buhman 1992] M. A. Arbib and J. Buhman, *Neural Networks*, **Encyclopedia of Artificial Intelligence** (2nd ed.), New York: John Wiley & Sons Inc., 1016-1060.

[Arbib 1964] M. A. Arbib, **Brains, Machines, and Mathematics**, New York: McGraw-Hill Book Company.

[Arbib 1985] M. A. Arbib, **In Search of the Person: Philosophical Explorations in Cognitive Science,** Amherst: The University of Massachusetts Press.

[Arbib 1987] M. A. Arbib, **Brains, Machines, and Mathematics** (2nd cd.), New York: Springer-Verlag.

[Arbib 1989] M. A. Arbib, **The Metaphorical Brains 2: Neural Networks and Beyond,** New York: Wiley Interscience.

[Arbib 1992] M. A. Arbib, *From Neurons to Minds via Schemas: Achieving Artificial Intelligence Through Cooperative Computation*, In [Morelli et.al.1992], 190-210.

[Arbib 1993] M. A. Arbib, Review of *A. Newell, Unified Theories of Cognition, **Artificial Intelligence**, 58: 265-283.

[Arbib 1995] M. A. Arbib (ed.), **The Handbook of Brain Theory** *and Neural Networks*, Cambridge: The MIT Press.

[Barwise & Feferman 1985] J. Barwise and S. Feferman (eds.), *Model-Theoretic Logics*, New York: Springer-Verlag.

[Barwise 1977] J. Barwise (ed.), *Handbook of Mathematical Logic*, Amsterdam: North-Holland Publishing Company.

[Barwise 1979] J. Barwise, *On Branching Quantifiers in English*, *Journal of Philosophical Logic*, 8: 47-80.

[Bechtel & Abrahamsen 1991] W. Bechtel and A. Abrahamsen, *Connectionism and the Mind: An Introduction to Parallel Processing in Networks*, Cambridge: Blackwell.

[Bechtel 1991] W. Bechtel, *Connectionism and the Philosophy of Mind: An Overview*, In [Horgan and Tienson 1991]

[Benacerraf 1967] P. Benacerraf, *God, the Devil, and Gödel, The Monist,* 51: 9-32.

[Benjafield 1992] J. G. Benjafield, *Cognition*, New Jersey: Prentice-Hall.

[Blaha 2005] S. Blaha, *The Equivalence of Elementary Particle Theories and Computer Languages: Quantum Computers, Turing Machines, Standard Model, Super String Theory, and a Proof that Gdel' Theorem Implies Nature Must be Quantum,* Auburn: Pingree-Hill Publishing.

[Birkhoff & von Neumann 1936] G. Birkhoff and J. von Neumann, "The Logic of Quantum Mechanics," *Annals of Mathematics* 37, No.4, 823-843.

[Bobrow 1994] D. Bobrow (ed.), *Artificial Intelligence in Perspective*, Cambridge: The MIT Press.

[Boden 1988] M. A. Boden, *Computer Models of Mind: Computational Approaches in Theoretical Psychology*,

Cambridge: Cambridge University Press.

[Boden 1993] M. A. Boden, *The Impact on Philosophy*, **The Simulation of Human Intelligence,** D. Broadbent (ed.), Oxford: Basil Blackwell Ltd.

[Bojadziev 1995] D. Bojadziev, *Gödel's Theorems for Minds and Computers*, **Informatica**, 19(4): 627-634.

[Boolos 1968] G. Boolos, *Review of Minds, Machines and Gödel, by* J. R. Lucas, *and God, the Devil, and Gödel, by* P. Benacerraf, **Journal of Symbolic Logic**, 33: 613-615.

[Boolos 1995] G. Boolos, *Introductory Note to Gödel 1951*, In [Gödel 1995], 290-304.

[Boyer 1983] D. L. Boyer, J. R. Lucas, Kurt Gödel, and Fred Astaire, **Philosophical Quarterly**, 33: 147-159.

[Bower & Clapper 1989] G. H. Bower and J. P. Clapper, *Experimental Methods in Cognitive Science*, **Foundations of Cognitive Science**, M. I. Posner (ed.), Cambridge: The MIT Press.

[Breuer 2001] T. Breuer, "Von Neumann, Gödel and Quantum Incompleteness", **John von Neumann and the Foundations of Quantum Physics**, M. Rédei and M. Stöltzner (eds.), Kluwer Academic Publishers.

[Carpenter & Grossberg 1995] G. A. Carpenter and S. Grossberg, *Adaptive Resonance Theory (ART)*, In [Arbib 1995], 79-82.

[Cenzer 1999] D. Cenzer, Π_1^0 *classes*, **Handbook of Computability Theory**, E. R. Griffor (ed.), Amsterdam: Elsevier, 37-85.

[Chaitin 1995] G. J. Chaitin, *Randomness in Arithmetic and the Decline and Fall of Reductionism in Pure Mathematics*, **Chaos, Solitons and Fractals**, 5(2): 143-159.

[Chalmers 1995] D. J. Chalmers, *Minds, Machines, and Mathematics*, **Psyche**, 2(9),

http://psyche.cs.monash.edu.au/v2/psyche.

[Chiara, Giuntini, & Rédei 2007] M. L. D. Chiara, R. Giuntini and M. Rédei, *The History of Quantum Logic*, **Handbook of the History of Logic**, Vol. 8, D. Gabbay and J. Woods (eds.), Elsevier.

[Chihara 1972] C. Chihara, *On Alleged Refutations of Mechanism Using Gödel's Incompleteness Results*, **Journal of Philosophy**, 69: 509-526.

[Church 1936] A. Church, *An Unsolvable Problem of Elementary Number Theory*, **American Journal of Mathematics**, 58: 345-363, In [Davis,1965].

[Churchland & Sejnowski 1989] P. S. Churchland and T. J. Sejnowski, *Neural Representation and Neural Computation*, In **Neural Connections, Mental Computations**, L. Nadel et al.(eds.), Cambridge: The MIT Press.

[Clark 1995] A. Clark, *Philosophical Issues in Brain Theory and Connectionism*, In [Arbib 1995], 738-741.

[Cleermans, Servan-Schreiber & McClelland 1989] A. Cleermans, D. Servan-Schreber, and J. L. McClelland, *Finite State Automata and Simple Recurrent Networks*, **Neural Computation**, 1: 372-381.

[Cole, Fetzer & Rankin 1990] D. J. Cole, J. H. Fetzer, and T. L. Rankin, **Philosophy, Mind, and Cognitive Inquiry: Resources for Understanding Mental Processes** Dordrecht: Kluwer.

[Copeland 1998] B. J. Copeland, *Turing's O-machine, Searle, Penrose, and the Brain*, **Analysis**, 58: 128-138.

[Cosnard 1995] M. Cosnard, *Parallel Computational Models*, In [Arbib 1995], 702-705.

[Cowan & Sharp 1988] J. D. Cowan & D. H. Sharp, *Neural Nets and Artificial Intelligence*, In [Graubard 1988], 85-122.

[Cummins & Schwarz] R. Cummins and G. Schwarz, *Connectionism, Computation, and Cognition*, In [Horgan and Tienson 1991].

[Cutland 1980] N. Cutland, **Computability: An Introduction to Recursive Function Theory**, Cambridge: Cambridge University Press.

[Davis 1958] M. Davis, **Computability and Unsolvability**, McGraw-Hill New York, reprinted in 1982, New York: Dover Publications.

[Davis 1965] M. Davis (ed.), **The Undecidable. Basic Papers on Undecidable Propositions, Unsolvable Problems, and Computable Functions**, New York: Raven Press.

[Davis 1982] M. Davis, *Why Gödel did not have Church's thesis*, **Information and Control,** 54: 3-24.

[Davis 1987] M. Davis, *Mathematical Logic and the Origin of Modern Computers*, In **Studies In the History of Mathematics**, E. R. Phillips (ed.), The Mathematical Association of America, 137-165.

[Dawson 1997] J. W. Dawson, Jr., **Logical Dilemmas: The Life and Work of Kurt Gödel**, Massachusetts A K Peters.

[DeLong 1970] H. DeLong, **A Profile of Mathematical Logic**, Massachusetts: Addison-Wesley.

[Dennett 1978] D. Dennett, **Brainstorms: Philosophical Essays on Mind and Psychology**, Cambridge: The MIT Press.

[Dennett 1988] D. Dennett, *When Philosophers Encounter Artificial Intelligence*, In [Graubard 1988], 283-296.

[Dreyfus & Dreyfus 1988] H. L. Dreyfus & S. E. Dreyfus, *Making a Mind versus Modeling the Brain: Artificial Intelligence Back at a Branchpoint*, In [Graubard 1988], 15-44.

[Dunn, Hagge, Moss, Wang 2005] J. Dunn, T. Hagge, L. Moss, L. & Z. Wang, Quantum Logic as Motivated by Quantum Computing. ***The Journal of Symbolic Logic.*** Vol. 70, No.2, 353-359.

[Dyer 1991] M. G. Dyer, *Connectionism versus Symbolism in High-Level Cognition*, In [Horgan and Tienson 1991].

[Ebbinghaus 1985] H. D. Ebbinghaus, *Extended Logics: The General Framework*, In [Barwise & Feferman 1985], 25-76.

[Enderton 1977] H. B. Enderton, *Elements of recursion theory*, In [Barwise,1977].

[Feferman & Solovay 1990] S. Feferman and R. M. Solovay, *Introductory Note to 1972a*, In [Gödel 1990], 281-292.

[Feferman 1962] S. Feferman, *Transfinite Recursive Progressions of Axiomatic Theories,* ***Journal of Symbolic Logic*** 27: 259-316.

[Feferman 1992] S. Feferman, *Turing's 'Oracle': From Absolute to Relative Computability,* ***The Space of Mathematics***, Berlin: Walter de Gruyter, 314-348.

[Feferman 1994] S. Feferman, *Turing in the Land of* , In [Herken 1994], 103-134.

[Feferman 1995] S. Feferman, *Penrose's Gödelian Argument,* ***Psyche***, 2(7), http://psyche.cs.monash.edu.au/v2/psyche.

[Feferman 1996] S. Feferman, *Gödel's Program for New Axioms: Why, Where, How and What?*, In ***Gödel '96***, Lecture Notes in Logic 6, 3-22.

[Feferman 1998] S. Feferman, *In the Light of Logic*, Oxford: Oxford University Press.

[Feldman & Ballard 1982] J. A. Feldman & D. H. Ballard, *Connectionist Models and Their Properties*, **Cognitive Science**, 6: 205-254.

[Fischler & Frischein, 1987] M. A. Fischler and O. Firschein, **Intelligence: The eye, the Brain, and the Computer**, Massachusetts Addison-Wesley Publishing Company.

[Flum 1985] J. Flum, *Characterizing Logics*, In [Barwise & Feferman 1985], 77-120.

[Fodor & Pylyshyn 1988] J. A. Fodor & Z. Pylyshyn, *Connectionism and Cognitive Architecture: A Critical Analysis*, **Cognition**, 28: 3-71.

[Franklin & Garzon 1991] S. Franklin and M. Garzon, *Neural Computability*, **Progress in Neural Networks,** vol.1, O. Omidvar (ed.), New Jersey: Ablex Publishing Corporation.

[Franklin & Garzon 1996] S. Franklin and M. Garzon, *Computation by Discrete Neural Nets*, In [Smolensky 1996].

[Franklin 1995] S. Franklin, **Artificial Minds**, Cambridge: The MIT Press.

[Gandy 1980] R. Gandy, *Church's Thesis and Principles for Mechanisms,* **The Kleene Symposium**, North-Holland, 123-148.

[Gandy 1996] R. Gandy, *Human versus Mechanical Intelligence*, In [Millican & Clark 1996], 125-136.

[Garson 1991] J. W. Garson, *What Connectionists Cannot Do: The*

Threat to Classical AI, In [Horgan and Tienson 1991].

[Garzon 1990] M. Garzon, *Cellular Automata and Discrete Neural Networks*, **Physica D** 45: 431-440.

[Garzon 1995] M. Garzon, **Models of Massive Parallelism: Analysis of Cellular Automata and Neural Networks**, Berlin: Springer-Verlag.

[Glymour 1991] C. Glymour, *The Hierarchies of Knowledge and the Mathematics of Discovery*, In [Millican & Clark 1996], 265-291.

[Good 1967] I. J. Good, *Human and Machine Logic*, **British Journal for the Philosophy of Science,** 18: 144-147.

[Good 1969] I. J. Good, *Gödel's Theorem is a Red Herring*, **British Journal for the Philosophy of Science,** 19: 357-358.

[Goodstein 1963] R. L. Goodstein, The Significance of Incompleteness Theorems, **British Journal for the Philosophy of Science,** 14: 208-220.

[Goertzel 1993] B. Goertzel, **The Structure of Intelligence: A New Mathematical Model of Mind,** New York: Springer-Verlag.

[Goertzel 1994] B. Goertzel, **Chaotic Logic: Language, Thought, and Reality from the Perspective of Complex Systems Science,** New York: Plenum Press.

[Graubard 1988] S. R. Graubard (ed.), **The Artificial Intelligence Debate: False Starts, Real Foundations**, Cambridge: The MIT Press.

[Green et al. 1996] D. W. Green et al., **Cognitive Science: An Introduction**, Oxford: Blackwell Publishers.

[Gödel 1931] K. Gödel, *On Formally Undecidable Propositions of Principia Mathematica and Related Systems I*, In [Gödel

1986].

[Gödel 1932] K. Gödel, *On Completeness and Consistency*, In [Gödel 1986].

[Gödel 1934] K. Gödel, *On Undecidable Propositions of Formal Mathematical Systems*, notes by S. C. Kleene and J. B. Rosser on lectures at the Institute for Advanced Study, Princeton, New Jersey, In [Gödel 1986].

[Gödel 1936] K. Gödel, *On the Length of Proofs*, In [Gödel 1986].

[Gödel 1940] K. Gödel, **The Consistency of the Axiom of Choice and of the Generalized Continuum Hypothesis**, Annals of Mathematics Studies No. 3, Princeton: Princeton University Press.

[Gödel 1946] K. Gödel, *Remarks before the Princeton Bicentennial Conference of Problems in Mathematics*, In [Gödel 1990].

[Gödel 1951] K. Gödel, *Some Basic Theorems on the Foundations of Mathematics and Their Implications*, In [Gödel 1995].

[Gödel 1963] K. Gödel, *Postscriptum to Gödel 1931*, In [Gödel 1986].

[Gödel 1964] K. Gödel, *Postscriptum to Gödel 1934*, In [Gödel 1986].

[Gödel 1972] K. Gödel, *Some Remarks on the Undecidability Results*, In [Gödel 1990].

[Gödel 1986] K. Gödel, **Collected Works volume I: Publications 1929-1936**, S.Feferman et al.(eds.), Oxford: Oxford University Press.

[Gödel 1990] K. Gödel, **Collected Works volume II: Publications 1938-1974**, S.Feferman et al.(eds.), Oxford: Oxford

University Press.

[Gödel 1995] K. Gödel, *Collected Works volume III: Unpublished Essays and Lectures,* S. Feferman et al.(eds.), Oxford: Oxford University Press.

[Hanson & Burr 1990] S. J. Hanson and D. Burr, *What Connectionist Models Learn: Learning and Representation in Connectionist Networks*, *Behavioral and Brain Science*s 13: 471-518.

[Hanson 1971] W. H. Hanson, *Mechanism and Gödel's Theorems*, *British Journal for the Philosophy of Science* 22: 9-16.

[Hatfield 1991] G. Hatfield, *Representation and Rule-Instantiation in Connectionist Systems*, In [Horgan and Tienson 1991].

[Haugeland 1981] J. Haugeland (ed.), *Mind Design*, Cambridge: The MIT Press.

[Hebb 1949] D. O. Hebb, *The Organization of Behavior*, New York: John Wiley & Sons.

[Henkin 1961] L. Henkin, *Some Remarks on Infinitely Long Formulas*, *Infinistic Methods*, 167-183.

[Herken 1994] R. Herken (ed.), *The Universal Turing Machine: A Half-Century Survey*, New York: Springer-Verlag.

[Hilbert 1927] D. Hilbert, *The Foundations of Mathematics*, In [van Heijenoort 1967], 464-479.

[Hiley 1997] B. Hiley, *Quantum Mechanics and the Relationship between Mind and Matter,* P. Pylkkanen et.al. *Brain, Mind and Physics,* Amsterdam: IOS Press.

[Hillis 1988] W. D. Hillis, *Intelligence as an Emergent Behavior; or, The Songs of Eden*, In [Graubard 1988], 175-190.

[Hintikka 1994] J. Hintikka, *Why Parallel Processing? **Philosophy*** *and the Cognitive Sciences*, R.Casati, B.Smith, and G.White (eds.), 265-272.

[Hofstadter 1979] D. R. Hofstadter, ***Gödel, Escher, Bach: An Eternal Golden Braid***, New York: Basic Books Inc.

[Hodgson 1991] D. Hodgson, ***The Mind Matters: Consciousness and Choice in a Quantum World***, Oxford: Oxford University Press.

[Holyoak & Spellman 1993] K. Holyoak and B. Spellman, *Thinking*, ***Annual Review of Psychology***, 44: 265-315.

[Hopcroft &Ullman 1979] J. E. Hopcroft and J.D. Ullman, ***Introduction to Automata Theory, Languages, and Computation,*** Massachusetts: Addison-Wesley Publishing Company.

[Horgan & Tienson 1991] T. Horgan and J. Tienson (ed.), ***Connectionism and the Philosophy of Mind***, Dordrecht: Kluwer.

[Horgan & Tienson 1996] T. Horgan and J. Tienson, ***Connectionism and the Philosophy of Psychology***. Cambridge: The MIT Press.

[Hurlbert & Poggio 1988] A. Hurlbert & T. Poggio, *Making Machines (and Artificial Intelligence) See*, In [Graubard 1988], 213-240.

[Hyun 2000] W. Hyun, ***Cognitive Computability and Gödel's Incompleteness: Cognitive Systems in Metamathematical Perspective***, Ph.D. Dissertation, Interdisciplinary Program in Cognitive Science, Yonsei University.

[Jaquette 1987] D. Jaquette, *Metamathematical Criteria for Minds and Machines,* ***Erkenntnis,*** 27: 1-16.

[Jech 1994] T. Jech, *On Gödel's Second Incompleteness Theorem*, **Proceeding of The American Mathematical Society,** 121: 311-313.

[Jech 1997] T. Jech, **Set Theory** (2nd ed.), Berlin: Springer-Verlag.

[Judd 1996] J. S. Judd, *Complexity of Learning*, In [Smolensky 1996].

[Kak 1992] S. Kak, *Can We Build a Quantum Neural Computer?* **Technical Report ECE/LSU 92-13,** Baton Rouge: Louisiana State University Electrical and Computer Engineering Department.

[King 1996] D. King, *Is the Human Mind a Turing Machine?* **Synthese,** 108(3): 379-389.

[Kirk 1986] R. Kirk, *Mental Machinery and Gödel,* **Synthese,** 66: 437-452.

[Kleene 1936] S. C. Kleene, *General Recursive Functions of Natural Numbers,* **MathematischeAnnalen** 112: 727-742, In [Davis, 1965].

[Kleene 1943] S. C. Kleene, *Recursive Predicates and Quantifiers,* **Transaction of the Ameriacn Mathematical Society,** 53: 41-73.

[Kleene 1952] S. C. Kleene, **Introduction to Metamathematics,** Princeton: D. Van Nostrand.

[Kleene 1956] S. C. Kleene, *Representation of Events in Nerve Nets and Finite Automata,* **Automata Studies,** C. E. Shanon and J. McCarthy (eds.), New Jersey: Princeton University Press, 3-41.

[Kleene 1994] S. C. Kleene, *Turing's Analysis of Computability, and Major Applications of It,* In: [Herken 1994], 15-49.

[Kohonen 1988] T. Kohonen, *An Introduction to Neural Computing,*

Neural Networks, 1: 3-16.

[Kreisel 1972] G. Kreisel, *Which Number-theoretic Problems can be Solved in Recursively Progressions on Π_1^1-paths thtough 0?* **The Journal of Symbolic Logic**, 37: 311-334.

[Kreisel 1974] G. Kreisel, *A Notion of Mechanistic Theory,* **Synthese**, 29: 11-26.

[LaForte, Hayes, & Ford 1998] G. LaForte, P. J. Hayes, and K. M. Ford, *Why Gödel's Theorem Cannot Refute Computationalism,* **Artificial Intelligence**, 104: 265-286.

[Lippmann 1987] R. P. Lippmann, *An Introduction to Computing with Neural Nets,* **IEEE Acoustics, Speech, and Signal Processing**, April, 4-22.

[Lockwood 1989] M. Lockwood, **Mind, Brain and the Quantum: The Compound I,** Cambridge: Blackwell.

[Lucas 1961] J. R. Lucas, *Minds, Machines, and Gödel,* **Philosophy**, 36: 112-137.

[Lucas 1996] J. R. Lucas, *Minds, Machines, and Gödel: A retrospect,* In [Millican and Clark 1996], 103-124.

[Luger 1995] G. F. Luger (ed.), **Computers and Intelligence: Collected Readings,** Cambridge, The MIT Press.

[Lyngzeidetson & Solomon 1994] A. E. Lyngzeidetson and M. K. Solomon, *Abstract Complexity Theory and the Mind-Machine Problem,* **British Journal for the Philosophy of Science**, 45: 549-554.

[Lyngzeidetson 1990] A. E. Lyngzeidetson, *Massively Parallel Distributed Processing and a Computationalist Foundation for Cognitive Science,* **British Journal for the Philosophy of Science**, 41: 121-127.

[Marr & Poggio 1979] D. Marr and T. Poggio, *A Computational Theory of Human Stereo Vision*, **Proceedings of the Royal Society of London**, 204: 301-328.

[Marr 1977] D. Marr, *Artificial Intelligence: A Personal View*, **Artificial Intelligence**, 9: 37-48.

[Marr 1982] D. Marr, **Vision**, New York: W.H.Freeman and Company.

[McCarthy 1988] J. McCarthy, *Mathematical Logic in Artificial Intelligence*, In [Graubard 1988], 297-311.

[McCarthy 1995] J. McCarthy, *Awareness and Understanding in Computer Programs*, **Psyche**, 2(11), http://psyche.cs.monash.edu.au/v2/psyche.

[McCarthy 1995] J. McCarthy, *Awareness and Understanding in Computer Programs*, **Psyche**, 2(11), http://psyche.cs.monash.edu.au/v2/psyche.

[McClelland, Rumelhart & Hinton 1986] J. L. McClelland, D. E. Rumelhart, and G. E. Hinton, *The Appeal of Parallel Distributed Processing*, **Parallel Distributed Processing. Explorations in the Microstructure of Cognition Volume I: Foundations,** D. E. Rumelhart and J. McClelland (eds.), Cambridge: The MIT Press.

[McCorduck 1988] P. McCorduck, *Artificial Intelligence: An Aperu*, In [Graubard 1988], 65-84.

[McCulloch & Pitts 1943] W. S. McCulloch and W. Pitts, *A logical calculus of the ideas immanent in nervous activity*, **Bulletin of Mathematical Biophysics**, 5: 115-133, In [Anderson and Rosenfeld,1988].

[Medler 1998] D. A. Medler, *A Brief History of Connectionism*,

Neural Computing Surveys, 1: 61-101.

[Millican & Clark 1996] P. Millican and A. Clark, ***Machines and Thought: The Legacy of Alan Turing, Volume I***, Oxford: Oxford University Press.

[Minsky & Papert 1988] M. Minsky and S. Papert, ***Perceptrons (Expanded Edition)***, Cambridge: The MIT Press.

[Minsky 1961] M. Minsky, *Steps Towards Artificial Intelligence*, In [Luger 1995], 47-90.

[Minsky 1967] M. Minsky, ***Computation: Finite and infinite machines,*** Englewood Cliffs: Prentice-Hall.

[Minsky 1985] M. Minsky, ***Society of Mind,*** New York: Simon and Schuster.

[Minsky 1991a] M. Minsky, *Logical Versus Analogical or Symbolic Versus Connectionist or Neat Versus Scruffy*, ***AI Magazine,*** 12(2): 52-69.

[Minsky 1991b] M. Minsky, *Machinery of Consciousness*, ***Proceedings of National Research Council of Canada, 7th Anniversary Symposium on Science in Society***.

[Morelli & Brown 1992] R. Morelli and W. M. Brown, *Computational Models of Cognition*, In [Morelli et.al. 1992], 1-35.

[Morelli et al. 1992] R. Morelli, W. M. Brown, D. Anselmi, K. Haberlandt, and D. Lloyd (ed.), ***Minds, Brains, and Computers: Perspectives in Cognitive Science and Artificial Intelligence***, New Jersey: Ablex Publishing Corporation.

[Moreno-Diaz & Mira 1996] R. Moreno-Diaz and J. Mira, Logic and Neural Nets: Variations on theme by W. S. McCulloch, ***Brain Processes, Theories, and Models: An International***

Conference in Honor of W. S. McCulloch 25 Years after His Death, R. Moreno-Diaz and J. Mira-Mira (eds.), Cambridge: The MIT Press, 24-36.

[Myhill 1964] J. Myhill, *The Abstract Theory of Self-Reproduction*, **Views on General Systems Theory,** M. D. Mesarovic (ed.), John Wiley and Sons, 106-118.

[Nagel and Newman 1958] E. Nagel and J. R. Newman, **Gödel's Proof,** New York: New York University Press.

[Nelson 1987] R. J. Nelson, *Church's Thesis and Cognitive Science,* **Notre Dame Journal of Formal Logic,** 28: 581-614.

[Newell & Simon 1976] A. Newell and H. A. Simon, *Computer Science as Empirical Inquiry: Symbols and Search,* **Communications of the Association for Computing Machinery**, 19: 113-126.

[Newell 1980] A. Newell, *Physical Symbol Systems,* **Cognitive Science**, 4: 135-183.

[Newell 1990] A. Newell, **Unified Theories of Cognition**, Cambridge: Harvard University Press.

[Newell 1992a] A. Newell, *Metaphors for Mind, Theories of Mind: Should the Humanities Mind?* In [Morelli et al. 1992], 95-133.

[Newell 1992b] A. Newell, *Prcis of Unified theories of cognition,* **Behavioral and Brain Sciences**, 15: 425-492.

[Norman 1981] D. A. Norman (ed.), **Perspectives on Cognitive Science**, New Jersey: Ablex Publishing Corporation.

[Norman 1981] D. A. Norman, *Twelve Issues for Cognitive Science,* In [Norman 1981], 265-295.

[Norman 1981] D. A. Norman, *What is Cognitive Science?* In

[Norman 1981], 1-11.

[Papert 1988] S. Papert, *One AI or Many?*, In [Graubard 1988], 1-14.

[Parberry 1994] I. Parberry, **Circuit Complexity and Neural Networks**, Cambridge: The MIT Press.

[Parberry 1995] I. Parberry, *Structural Complexity and Discrete Neural Networks,* In [Arbib 1995], 945-948.

[Parberry 1996] I. Parberry, *Circuit Complexity and Feedforward Neural Networks*, In [Smolensky 1996], 85-111.

[Penrose 1989] R. Penrose, **The Emperor's New Mind**, Oxford: Oxford University Press.

[Penrose 1990] R. Penrose, *Precis of The Emperor's New Mind: Concerning Computers, Minds, and the Laws of Physics*, **Behavioral and Brain Sciences**, 13: 643-705.

[Penrose 1993a] R. Penrose, *Setting the Scene: the Claim and the Issues, **The Simulation of Human Intelligence,** * D. Broadbent (ed.), Oxford: Blackwell.

[Penrose 1993b] R. Penrose, *An Emperor Still Without Mind*, **Behavioral and Brain Sciences**, 16: 616-622.

[Penrose 1994] R. Penrose, **Shadows of the mind**, Oxford: Oxford University Press.

[Penrose 1996] R. Penrose, *Beyond the Doubting of a Shadow,* **Psyche**, 2(23), http://psyche.cs.monash.edu.au/v2/psyche.

[Penrose 1997] R. Penrose, **The Large, the Small and the Human Mind**, Cambridge: Cambridge University Press.

[Port & van Gelder 1995] F. F. Port and T. van Gelder (ed.), **Mind as Motion: Explorations in the Dynamics of Cognition**, Cambridge: The MIT Press.

[Post 1936] E. Post, *Finite Combinatory Processes, Formulation 1*, **Journal of Symbolic Logic**, 1: 103-105, In [Davis 1965].

[Post 1965] E. Post, *Absolutely Unsolvable Problems and Relatively Undecidable Propositions: Account of an Anticipation*, In [Davis, 1965]

[Pour-El 1996] M. B. Pour-El, *The Mathematical Theory of the Analog Computer*, In [Smolensky 1996].

[Putnam 1964] H. Putnam, *Minds and Machines*, In **Minds and Machines**, A. R. Anderson (ed.), Englewood Cliffs: Prentice-Hall, 72-97.

[Putnam 1995] *Book Reviews of Shadows of the mind, by Roger Penrose*, **Bulletin of the American Mathematical Society**, 32(3): 370-373.

[Pylyshyn 1984] Z. W. Pylyshyn, **Computation and Cognition**, Cambridge: The MIT Press.

[Pylyshyn 1989] Z. W. Pylyshyn, *Computing in Cognitive Science*, **Foundations of Cognitive Science**, M. I. Posner (ed.), Cambridge: The MIT Press.

[Reeke, Jr. & Edelman 1988] G. N. Reeke, Jr. and G. M. Edelman, *Real Brains and Artificial Intelligence*, In [Graubard 1988], 143-174.

[Rheinwald 1991] R. Rheinwald, *Mind, Machines and Gödel's Theorem*, **Erkenntnis,** 31: 1-21.

[Rolls 1993] E. T. Rolls, *Networks in the Brain*, In **The Simulation of Human Intelligence,** D. Broadbent (ed.), Oxford: Basil Blackwell Ltd.

[Rosenblatt 1959] F. Rosenblatt, **Principles of Neurodynamics**, New York: Spartan.

[Rosmaita 1995] B. J. Rosmaita, ***Metamathematics and Mind: The Implications of Undecidability Results for Theories of Human Cognition***, Ph. D. Dissertation, Dept. of Philosophy, The University of Notre Dame.

[Rucker 1995] R. Rucker, ***Infinity and the Mind: The Science and Philosophy of the Infinite***, New Jersey: Princeton University Press.

[Rueckl 1991] J. G. Rueckl, *Connectionism and the Notion of Levels*, In [Horgan and Tienson 1991].

[Rumelhart & McClelland 1986] D. E. Rumelhart, J. L. McClelland, and the PDP Research Group, ***Parallel Distributed Processing: Explorations in the Microstructure of Cognition, vol.1: Foundations***, The MIT Press, Cambridge.

[Rumelhart 1989] D. E. Rumelhart, *The Architecture of Mind: A Connectionist Approach*, In ***Foundations of Cognitive Science,*** M. I. Posner (ed.), Cambridge: The MIT Press, 133-159.

[Rumelhart, Hinton, & McClelland 1986] D. E. Rumelhart, G. E. Hinton, and J. L. McClelland, *A General Framework for Parallel Distributed Processing*, In [Rumelhart & McClelland 1986], 45-76.

[Rumelhart, Hinton, & Williams 1986] D. E. Rumelhart, G. E. Hinton, and R. J. Williams, *Learning internal representations by error propagation*, In [Rumelhart, McClelland 1986], 318-362.

[Schwartz 1988] J. T. Schwartz, *The New Connectionism: Developing Relationships Between Neuroscience and Artificial Intelligence*, In [Graubard 1988], 123-142.

[Shankar 1994] N. Shankar, *Metamathematics, Machines, and Gödel's Proof,* New York: Cambridge University Press.

[Shanker 1988] S. G. Shanker, *Gödel's Theorem in Focus*, London: Routledge.

[Shapiro 1998] S. Shapiro, *Incompleteness, Mechanism, and Optimism*, *The Bulletin of Symbolic Logic*, 4(3): 273-302.

[Sieg 1994] W. Sieg, *Mechanical Procedures and Mathematical Experience, Mathematics and mind,* A. George (ed.), Oxford: Oxford University Press.

[Siegelman & Sontag 1991] H. T. Siegelman and E. D. Sontag, *Turing computability with Neural Nets, Applied Mathematics Letters,* 4(6): 77-80.

[Siegelman & Sontag 1994] H. T. Siegelman and E. D. Sontag, *Analog Computation via Neural Networks, Theoretical Computer Science,* 131: 331-360.

[Siegelman & Sontag 1995] H. T. Siegelman and E. D. Sontag, *On the Computational Power of Neural Networks, Journal of Computer and System Sciences*, 50(1): 132-155.

[Siegelman 1999] H. T. Siegelmann, *Neural Networks and Analog Computation: Beyond Turing Machine*, Boston: Birkhuser.

[Simon & Kaplan 1989] H. A. Simon and C. A. Kaplan, *Foundations of Cognitive Science, In Foundations of Cognitive Science,* M.I.Posner (ed.), Cambridge: The MIT Press.

[Simon 1995] H. A. Simon, *Machine as Mind*, In [Millican & Clark 1996], 81-102.

[Slezak 1982] P. Slezak, *Gödel's Theorem and the mind, British Journal for the Philosophy of Science,* 33: 41-52.

[Sloman 1996] A. Sloman, *Beyond Turing Equivalence*, In [Millican & Clark 1996], 179-219.

[Smart 1961] J. J. C. Smart, *Gödel's Theorem, Church's Theorem and Mechanism*, **Synthese**, 13: 105-110.

[Smolensky 1988] P. Smolensky, *On the Proper Treatment of Connectionism*, **Behavioral and Brain Sciences**, 11: 1-74.

[Smolensky 1996a] P. Smolensky, *Computational, Dynamical, and Statistical Perspectives on the Processing and Learning Problems in Neural Network Theory*, In [Smolensky 1996].

[Smolensky 1996b] P. Smolensky, *Computational Perspectives on Neural Networks*, In [Smolensky 1996]

[Smolensky et al. 1996] P. Smolensky, M. C. Mozer, and D. E. Rumelhart (eds), **Mathematical Perspectives on Neural networks**, New Jersey: Lawrence Erlbaum Associates.

[Smorynski 1977] C. Smorynski, *The Incompleteness Theorems*, In [Barwise,1977].

[Soare 1987] R. I. Soare, **Recursively Enumerable Sets and Degrees**, Springer Verlag, New York.

[Soare 1996] R. I. Soare, *Computability and Recursion*, **The Bulletin of Symbolic Logic**, 2(3): 284-321.

[Soare 1999] R. I. Soare, *The History and Concept of Computability*, **Handbook of Computability Theory**, E. R. Griffor (ed.), Amsterdam: Elsevier, 3-36.

[Sokolowski 1988] R. Sokolowski, *Natural and Artificial Intelligence*, In [Graubard 1988], 45-64.

[Sontag 1995] E. D. Sontag, *Automata and Neural Networks*, In [Arbib 1995], 119-123.

[Statman 1978] R. Statman, *Bounds for Proof-search and Speed-up in the Predicate Calculus*, **Annals of mathematical logic**, 15: 225-287.

[Stapp 2004] H. Stapp, **Mind, Matter and Quantum Mechanics,** (2nd ed.). Berlin: Springer-Verlag.

[Statman 1982] R. Statman, *Speed-up by Theories with Infinite Models*, **Proceedings of the American Mathematical Society**, 81: 465-469.

[Tamburrini 1987] G. Tamburrini, **Reflections on Mechanism**, Ph.D. Dissertation, Columbia University.

[Tamburrini 1995] G. Tamburrini, *Mechanistic Theories in Cognitive Science: The Import of Turing's Thesis*, **Proceedings of the 10th International Congress of Logic, Methodology, and Philosophy of Science**, 1995, Florence.

[Turing 1936] A. M. Turing, *On Computable Numbers, with an Application to the Entscheidungsproblem*, **Proceedings of the London Mathematical Society**, 42: 230-265, In [Davis 1965], 116-151.

[Turing 1939] A. M. Turing, *Systems of Logic Based on Ordinals*, **Proceedings of the London Mathematical Society**, ser 2, 45: 161-228, In [Davis 1965], 155-222..

[Turing 1950] A. M. Turing, *Computing Machinery and Intelligence*, **Mind**, 59: 433-460.

[Vapnik 1995] V. Vapnik, *Learning and Generalization: Theoretical Bounds*, In [Arbib 1995], 516-522.

[Varela et al. 1991] F. J. Varela, E. Thompson, and E. Rosch, **The Embodied Mind: Cognitive Science and Human Experience**, Cambridge: The MIT Press.

[Waltz 1988] D. L. Waltz, *The Prospects for Building Truly Intelligent Machines*, In [Graubard 1988], 191-212.

[Wang 1974] H. Wang, **From Mathematics to Philosophy**, London: Routledge and Kegan Paul.

[Wang 1996] H. Wang, **A Logical journey: From Gödel to Philosophy**, Cambridge: The MIT Press.

[Webb 1968] J. Webb, *Metamathematics and the Philosophy of Mind*, **Philosophy of Science,** 35: 156-178.

[Webb 1980] J. Webb, **Mechanism, Mentalism and Metamathematics: An Essay on Finitism**, Dordrecht: D. Reidel.

[Webb 1990] J. Webb, *Introductory Note to 1972a*, In [Gödel 1990], 292-304.

[Werbos 1995] P. J. Werbos, *Backpropagation: Basics and New Developments*, In [Arbib 1995], 134-139.

[Whitely 1962] C. H. Whitely, *Minds, Machines, and Gödel: A Reply to Mr. Lucas*, **Philosophy** 37.

[Widrow and Lehr 1990] B. Widrow and M. A. Lehr, *30 Years of Adaptive Neural Networks: Perceptron, Madaline, and Backpropagation*, **Proceedings of the IEEE**, 78(9): 1415-1442.

[Widrow and Lehr 1995] B. Widrow and M. A. Lehr, *Perceptrons, Adalines, and Backpropagation*, In [Arbib 1995], 719-724.

[Williams 1986] R. J. Williams, *The Logic of Activation Functions*, In: [Rumelhart and McClelland 1986], 423-443.

[Williamson 1996] T. Williamson, *Self-Knowledge and Embedded Operators*, **Analysis,** 56: 202-209.

[Wright 1995] C. Wright, *Intuitionists Are Not (Turing) Machines*, **Philosophia Mathematica,** *3:* 86-102.

[Yu 1992] Q. Yu, *Consistency, Mechanicalness, and the Logic of Mind,* **Synthese,** 90: 145-179.

[van Heijenoort 1967] J. van Heijenoort, **From Frege to Gödel: A Source Book in Mathematical Logic, 1879-1931**, Cambridge: Harvard University Press.

[van Fraasen 1981] B. van Fraassen, *Assumption and Interpretations of Quantum Logic,* **Current Issues in Quantum Logic**, E. G. Beltrametti and B. van Fraassen (eds.), Plenum Press.